FINDING
GOD
WHEN LIFE'S
NOT FAIR

Lee Ezell is a gifted author and speaker. She has made us laugh for years. In this book Lee lays bare her soul and puts words to the questions we all long to ask but are afraid to. This is not a book of theory—she has walked every painful step and out of the struggles of her own life gives us this wonderful gift.

SHEILA WALSH, RECORDING ARTIST

Lee Ezell has graciously endured the blast furnace of the Refiner's fire. In *Finding God When Life's Not Fair*, Lee plants seeds of hope in the hearts of a society of sufferers. If your heart is hurting—read this book!

DR. JOHN C. HAGEE, PASTOR

Only Lee Ezell could take the subject of loss and approach it with humor and a deep sensitivity that grabs at your heart. Lee's words on pain and suffering ring true—she lives her talk. I know because Jan and I walked alongside her through the pain she describes. Lee never minimized the reality and pain of her losses, but at the same time, she never minimizes the power and presence of God's hand on her throughout it all. Here's a book that will bring God's light into your darkest times!

DAVID STOOP, PH.D., CLINICAL PSYCHOLOGIST, AUTHOR

Lee Ezell has proven herself over and over again as a woman who draws strength from the Scriptures in the face of tragedy and pain. The Word has been her salvation in many of the challenges she has faced in her life. Similarly, we can draw strength and comfort from *Finding God When Life's Not Fair*, as she continually points us to her comfort "with the comfort by which we have been comforted" (2 Cor. 1:4).

ANNA HAYFORD

FINDING GOD WHEN LIFE'S NOT FAIR

SURVIVING SOUL-SHAKERS
AND AFTERSHOCKS

LEE EZELL

Fleming H. Revell
A Division of Baker Book House Co
Grand Rapids, Michigan 49516

Published by Fleming H. Revell
a division of Baker Book House Company
P.O. Box 6287, Grand Rapids, MI 49516-6287

Fourth printing, April 2003

Printed in the United States of America

Library of Congress Cataloging-in-Publication Data

Ezell, Lee.
    Finding God when life's not fair : surviving soul-shakers and after-
shocks / Lee Ezell.
        p.   cm.
    Includes bibliographical references.
    ISBN 0-8007-5748-3
    1. Cancer—Religious aspects—Christianity. 2. Cancer—Patients—
Religious life. 3. Ezell, Lee. I. Title.

BV4910.33 .E94 2001
248.8′6—dc21   2001019420

For current information about all releases from Baker Book House, visit our web site:
http://www.bakerbooks.com

This book is dedicated,
with much love,
to my dear Hal.
Only the Holy Spirit
can replace you in being
the Wind beneath my wings.

CONTENTS

ACKNOWLEDGMENTS

You've all been so faithful in my hour of need. How can I ever say thanks? I hope you all know how very much I love and appreciate you!

The Ezell clan, especially Pam and Jim; Sandi, Rich, and Mason Bushnell; Don and Linda; Nana, and Velma and John.

Julie Makimaa.

The Harvey clan, especially Margaret.

Ryan and Gerda Audagnotti, Pam and Rich Boyer, Paul and Toni Danchik, Danny Darling, Stephen and Arlene Fleishman, Ron and Connie Haus, Susie Jones, Pat and Bill King, Clyde and Peggy Martin, Regis and Deb, Pat Rexroat, Pam and Mike Rozell, Daryl and Jennifer Silberberg, Betty and Fred Southard, Gisela and Steven B. Stevens, Dave and Jan Stoop, Jim and Norma Swanson, Bob and Laura Whyley.

Special thanks to my talented editor, Dave Wimbish. Without his expertise, writing this book would have been "unfair." Thanks, Dave.

PREFACE

Before we begin, it's only fair to warn you: I'm biased. I believe that the only true expression of God and His ways is found through the Holy Scriptures. This book is based on the premise that the reader also accepts the Bible as the Word of God—as His love letter and instruction manual for His kids.

All my assumptions and deductions are based on what this Holy Book has to say about God and His Son, Jesus Christ. If you are not sure about all this "religious" stuff, I encourage you to keep reading anyway, because I believe you will find healing in these pages.

FOR THE SURVIVAL-CHALLENGED

*Life is lived forward
and understood backward.*

Sad!

That's what I thought when I first saw her.

She was standing near the back of a long line of people who were waiting to talk to me after a speaking engagement.

She was a tall, attractive woman on the young side of middle age.

I would have guessed that she was in her late thirties.

Until I looked into her eyes.

They looked older, sadder somehow. Out of place in that otherwise pretty face.

If it's true that the eyes are a window to the soul, then I was looking into a soul that was well acquainted with sorrow.

When her place in the line finally reached me, she told me she was pleased to meet me, and then said, "You know, you're really amazing."

"I am?" I smiled, trying not to look too pleased. "What makes you think so?"

"Because," she sighed, "I know you've been through a lot, but you never seem to get mad at God."

"Oh, let me tell you . . ." I began, but she didn't give me a chance to finish my sentence.

"I mean, haven't you ever felt like shouting at Him? Or maybe shaking your fist and telling Him it's not fair?"

"You better believe I have!" I cried. "In fact, anyone who thinks I never got mad at God doesn't know me very well! Of course I got mad! And you bet I asked Him why crummy things happened to me!"

"Really!" she said. "So you don't think it's wrong to be angry with God?"

"Listen," I said, laughing, "if it's a sin to get upset with God, then we're probably all in a lot of trouble! We can get angry and not sin."

I can't say that it was that woman's question that prompted me to write this book. I'd already been thinking about it for quite a while. But she, and others like her, have helped me not to give up on this project when it started to feel "too heavy." They've let me know that it's important to keep going for the sake of thousands of Christians who have no idea what to do with their pain and grief, and who can't really admit the way they're feeling because they're afraid that to do so would be to commit a sin.

I'VE NEVER BEEN A MOURNING PERSON

Your experience of loss and pain may not be the same as mine. But if you have suffered—and you probably wouldn't be reading this book if you haven't—you realize that tragedy affects one's view of the universe in deep and lasting ways. When life seems unfair, no honest person will simply plaster a smile on her face and turn to God in easy, childlike trust.

No way! At one time or another, almost all of us will wonder how a loving God can allow such terrible suffering to fall upon the people He created.

Prior to the past few years, I had always considered myself to be a happy-go-lucky, lighthearted gal. I've never been a "mourning person." When it comes to life's problems, my philosophy has always been, "get over it . . . get a grip . . . get on with it."

Whatever came my way, I knew it was okay. I learned early in life that God truly is in charge of the universe, and Romans 8:28 is speaking the truth when it promises that God will cause all things to work together for the good of those who love Him. That wasn't something I learned by reading the Bible either. I had experienced this time and again in my own life.

Now, if you know me, you know that I'm not a stranger to pain and sorrow.

I'll tell you more of my story later on, but for now I'll just say that I've hurt, I've ached, I've cried. But in all of those times I've seen God work good—sooner or later.

Still, I was totally unprepared for the avalanche of trouble that descended upon my husband, Hal, and me two years ago now. Before that happened, I thought I had God pretty well figured out. After all, I'd written some best-selling books in which I'd talked passionately about my faith in Christ. I'd spoken to hundreds of thousands of people all over the world, encouraging them and exhorting them to live for God. I ought to know a thing or two.

But when my safe, comfortable life began to crumble, I found myself behaving like the Old Testament prophet Jeremiah—mentally shaking my fist at God and asking questions like: "Where are you?" "Don't you care anymore?" "If you're really in control of everything, how can you let this happen?" My relationship with God was shaken, and my understanding of His ways seemed hopelessly confused.

I felt like someone whose house had been ransacked by burglars. As if I had gone out in the morning with everything neatly in place and come home to find that all my possessions had been dumped onto the floor in a confusing, jumbled mess. It didn't seem to me that I would ever be able to get things back into the tidy little packages where they belonged. I longed to return to the ordinary world but could not seem to find my way.

PLANTING SEEDS OF HOPE

It's not my intention to tell some soap-opera sob story. We've all heard enough sad stories. My hope and prayer is that, through sharing examples of "unfairness" from my own life, I might drop some seeds of hope into other hurting hearts.

Believe me, there is no great blessing in having the experiences necessary to write a book on suffering! I certainly never wanted to write a book like this. I only wanted to write lighthearted books that would help people feel better about themselves and help them improve their relationships with each other and with God.

But I've discovered that for far too many people, there is a big gap between what they expect of God and what they experience. Many suffer from dashed expectations—what the Bible calls "hope deferred"—and wind up heartsick.

In this book, I will examine many of the promises that God makes to those who trust in Him and try to reconcile those promises with the disappointments that many of us feel so often. Now, I'm no theologian. If any real theologian reads these pages, he or she may cringe over how simplistically I've approached some heavy and complex topics. Yes, I am an amateur, but I am an amateur who has sincerely sought God for His answers to these difficult questions, and in these pages I will offer you what I have learned.

I can't say that I've come up with "answers." More like clues and hints and implications from which you, dear reader, must draw your own conclusions. This is my puny effort, as a layperson, to wrestle with questions about God and His dealings with His people—to bring them down out of the stained-glass theological sanctuary into the coffee-shop level where most people struggle with life.

I realize that I'm standing on some pretty shaky ground when I try to explain the actions (or lack thereof) of the Almighty. But perhaps, together, we can come to an understanding of how a God who loves us so very much often seems to stand by silently and watch without lifting a finger to help when life's tragedies threaten to bury us alive.

THE SOCIETY OF SUFFERERS

I can see now that even as I was struggling through the darkest, most distressing time I've ever known, God was working on me—molding me and shaping me ever more closely into the image of His Son. His Son, who prayed in the Garden of Gethsemane, "If it is possible, may this cup be taken from me." And who cried out as He hung on the cross, "My God, my God, why have you forsaken me?"

I have become more compassionate, less judgmental, more willing to listen, and less likely to give pat answers to people in pain who deserve better.

I have also become more aware that there is an entire subculture of people who are in pain. Sort of a "Society of Sufferers." You might call them "the survival-challenged."

As I've traveled and spoken around the world, I've heard their stories:

- The father in South Africa who couldn't understand why God would let his precious son drown.
- The mother in Michigan whose rebellious son was breaking her heart and her spirit.

17

- A family from the Midwest who told me how their home was totally demolished in seconds by a tornado, destroying everything they had worked so hard for so long to build.
- A woman in Dallas who was about to give birth to twins when she received word that her husband and mother had been killed in a car crash on their way to the hospital—a car crash caused by a drunken driver.

These are just some of the agonized faces that come to my mind when I think of the Society of Sufferers. This society includes people from all walks of life. No religious or racial group is excluded. It touches Christians, atheists, and people of all other religions. Surely, as Jesus said, the rain falls on the just and unjust alike (see Matt. 5:45).

Until recently, I could only hug these folks, pray and weep with them, and hope for the best. But I had no clue what was going on inside them—no idea of the extent of the pain that tore at their hearts. Often, I would think about their stories, marvel that they had ever been able to make it through, and wonder how I would react if I had to endure the same trials and tribulations.

There are hundreds of reasons why people are drawn into this group of the survival-challenged. Some are suffering from terminal or debilitating illnesses. Some are dealing with the loss of a spouse, child, or other loved one. Others have been through divorce, suffered financial reversal, or are dealing with chronic depression or other emotional difficulties. It's impossible to say whose loss is greater, or who suffers the most. Is divorce worse than the death of a spouse? There is no value in comparing one person's grief and loss to another person's sorrow. Life's injustices are dealt out daily, in the court system, in the medical profession, and through all kinds of betrayal and disappointment.

The question is not, "Who hurts most?" but rather, "What can be done to help us deal with our pain?" Some people try to cope by numbing their pain with pills, alcohol, or work. Some try to withdraw from the world. Others become loud and angry. Many look for answers in distorted religious systems or cults. And, sadly, some turn their backs on God, believing that He has let them down.

The truth is that people can't possibly know how they will respond to suffering until they are plunged into the fire. And my turn in the fire would come soon enough. When it did, I found myself clinging to the promise in the Book of Hebrews that God will give "grace to help us in our time of need" (4:16). But as I tried to hold on to Him in my time of suffering, it seemed to me that He was in no hurry to dispense that grace. I never expected to feel so stranded, so unable to find my way back to spiritual sanity. I felt as though I were bleeding internally, my faith becoming weak and anemic as a result. How often I wondered when I would find relief!

Recently, when a woman heard about the things I've been through, she remarked, "Your life sounds like a soap opera." I'm not a big fan of the soaps, but as I thought about it, I realized that the lady had a point. So I wrote this poem:

> I was raised in *Dark Shadows*,
> suffering *Northern Exposure*.
> And *As the World Turns*
> I would spend the *Days of Our Lives*
> Seeking to become one of
> *The Bold and the Beautiful*,
> But only became one of
> *The Young and the Restless*.
>
> In a desperate *Search for Tomorrow*
> I headed out for *Another World*,
> But instead ended up on
> *The Edge of Night* in *General Hospital*.
>
> Then Jesus Christ, my *Guiding Light*,
> Brought me through my *Secret Storm*.

19

> He said, "Come share with Me in My *Dynasty*,
> Become one of *All My Children*
> And I will give you *One Life to Live*."

Do you know what it's like to belong to this brotherhood of pain? If so, I am writing this book for you.

Perhaps someone dear to you has suffered, or is suffering, and you are looking for answers. Then again, I am writing for you.

Or perhaps you're simply troubled by the fact that there is so much pain and sorrow in the world and want to understand why. If so, I am writing for you.

But I am not writing to give you easy answers, because they don't exist.

I'm not writing to tell you why people suffer, because I don't know.

Nor can I promise that I will answer all of your questions about suffering, for, as C. S. Lewis wrote, "You can't see anything properly while your eyes are blurred with tears."

My intention is not to write a textbook on suffering, but rather, to take a journey in which we can hopefully discover the grace of God that is always available to us—even when we're sitting in the darkness of the storm cellar, listening to a tornado rip the house apart upstairs!

I hope that my honest questioning, conducted in an atmosphere of faith, will be of help to you as you struggle for relief in your own suffering—whether you are openly mourning or privately festering, having learned to cover your feelings well.

Before we begin that journey, there are three important points I want to make:

1. You may never "get over it." There was a time when I wondered when I was going to "get over" all the things that had gone wrong in my life. But today, I realize that it is unrealistic to believe people can simply "recover" from great loss and disillusionment.

I don't expect to ever get to the point where I feel like I did before my husband fell ill and before subsequent tragedies entered my life. Lee Ezell is a different woman today than she was two or three years ago.

But some people still want me to be the old Lee. They try to fix me by urging me to "just get on with your life." Anyone who has suffered deeply knows it's not that simple. The truth is: You may never get over it, but you can get through it!

I'm doing relatively well today. I'm clothed and in my right mind (as much as can be expected). But it's not because I'm such a strong woman, but because God allowed me a time of questioning, a time in which new life was born out of my loss.

You may never get over it, but you can get through it!

In the pages ahead, you'll see my faults and failures as I struggled to hold on to my faith during the darkest days. But I know now that courage can grow out of fear, and as a result, my faith is stronger today than before the foundations of my life were shaken so violently.

2. *The journey we're about to undertake leads to freedom.* This trip is not for the fainthearted, nor for those who want to keep believing that bad things simply don't happen to people who are close to God.

For Christians, suffering can be made even worse by the fact that so many of our fellow believers seem to have never read the Book of Job. Or if they read it, they didn't get it. If you're going through a rough time, they look at you as if there must be some secret sin in your life.

As a result, aching Christians often fall under condemnation, wondering what they have done that has caused the Lord to turn His back on them.

Or else they put plastic smiles on their faces, showing the world a happy, joyous facade, when they're dying inside. As a result, they don't get the help they need to get through their difficult times, and the pain grows deeper and becomes more difficult to overcome.

What a tragedy! The Book of Galatians says that Christians ought to bear one another's burdens. Instead, I've heard it said that Christians are the only people who shoot their wounded, and in some cases, I believe it's true.

3. *God is in charge, and He loves us.* Your experience of loss and pain may be different from mine. But you probably realize, as I do now, that tragedy affects one's view of the universe in deep and lasting ways. When life seems unfair, no honest person will simply plaster a smile on her face and turn to God in easy, childlike trust. How can we do that when we feel that our trust has been so violated?

So . . . am I a cynic now?

Absolutely not!

I have more hope now than I ever had before. But I did not arrive at this hope easily. As I tried to make sense out of the devastating events that had taken hold in my life, I found myself wrestling with difficult questions about God and His nature. Easy answers and platitudes simply wouldn't do. I wanted the answers to questions like:

- Is our death really in God's hands?
- Is it possible to know what heaven is like?

- Are our days really numbered, and if so, then what difference can prayer possibly make?
- What good does it do to pray when things only seem to be getting worse?
- Shouldn't there be some reward this side of heaven for living a dedicated life of faith?
- What possible good can come out of this situation?
- Is suffering random and senseless?

The more I have wrestled with questions like these, the more I have come to understand that God has never promised His people that their lives will be free from suffering.

God's hands that reach out to us don't extend to wound us, but they are wounded hands—nail-scarred hands.

He does promise that He will be with us when we suffer.

You can be sure that God loves you and is not punishing you by causing you to suffer. You're not paying off any "debt" you owe Him for sins you've committed. He already paid the debt we owe by sending His own Son to suffer and die in our behalf.

Always remember, God's hands that reach out to us don't extend to wound us, but they are wounded hands—nail-scarred hands.

I know, with complete certainty, that God cares and that He doesn't mind if we ask all the tough questions about suffering. Or anything else, for that matter!

In fact, at the end of each chapter you'll find a page we'll call "Asking . . . and Acting." James 1:5 says, "If any of you lacks wisdom, he should ask God, who gives generously to all without finding fault." Sometimes faith is gained by asking God tough questions and being willing to hear His answers, even if they're not what we want to hear.

But that's not all we must do, as James points out in the next chapter. He mentions Abraham as a stellar example of a man with faith, and then says: "You see that his faith and his actions were working together." Then he adds that Abraham's "faith was made complete by what he did" (v. 22). Asking. Acting. They work together to produce faith!

"Asking . . . and Acting!" is designed to help you ask some important questions as you go through your process of healing. I will also suggest some actions that will aid the healing process. My prayer is that the ultimate return for you will be growth through your grief. That will make it a priceless treasure in your life rather than a painful waste of time.

Are you ready for the journey? Then let's go!

Asking . . . and Acting!

Step 1: Asking

Is personal pain creating a gap between you and God or helping you draw closer to Him?

Step 2: Acting

Make a list below of the things you hope to gain from reading this book. I'll get you started:

1. Growth
2. Grace for the journey
3.
4.
5.

For Bible Study

Matthew 5:45
Romans 8:28
Hebrews 4:16
James 1:5, 22

TWO

DEALING WITH THE "BIG C"

Through many dangers, toils and snares,
I have already come;
'Tis grace hath brought me safe thus far,
And grace will lead me home.

John Newton

Loveable.

That's the first word that comes to mind when I think of my husband, Hal.

And that's not just my opinion. He was just one of those good guys who everybody liked and most loved.

Because he was a big guy, he could seem intimidating when you first met him. But if you spent any time with him at all, it didn't take very long to see his soft and sensitive side.

We met at a Bible conference and, even though it may sound like a romantic cliché, it really was "love at first sight." We began dating, and the more I got to know him, the more my feelings grew. I was especially touched by the tender way he related to his two daughters, Pamela and Sandra.

Hal certainly knew something about suffering. He had been married twice, to two beautiful Christian women. The first died from a brain tumor, the second with lupus.

I was thrilled when Hal asked me to become his third wife. After all, third time's a charm, you know . . . and last certainly doesn't mean least!

After serving in President Reagan's administration as Commissioner of Immigration for the Western Region, Hal opened his own business. There wasn't a risk in the world that could scare him. He was bold and brave and enthusiastic. I wouldn't be surprised to find his photograph in the dictionary, right next to the word *entrepreneur*.

He had never been the sickly type. Never one to run to the doctor because he didn't feel well. He just kept on going, figuring that he'd charge through any illness and come out safe on the other side.

ZAPPED BY GOD

Hal had always been very interested in the healing ministry. And so it was that one beautiful autumn evening found me sitting very near the front row in a healing crusade being conducted by a famous evangelist.

I really didn't want to be there. Frankly, there was something about this particular evangelist that bugged me. Big time! It wasn't that he said anything that dishonored God. He was always ready to give the glory for everything that happened through his ministry to Jesus Christ. But I felt that some of his mannerisms were over-the-top—more suited for a Las Vegas lounge act than a church service.

Nevertheless, I sat there trying not to be distracted by his personality or his appearance, focusing instead on his Bible-based message.

Near the end of the service, the evangelist looked out into the audience and said, "If you want more power for ministry, I want you to come up to the stage right now and let me pray for you."

Well, why not? I figured I might as well join the dozens of other people who were on their way to the front of the auditorium. After all, prayer couldn't hurt. It's also true that traveling around the country, speaking night after night for long periods of time, can be exhausting. More power for ministry? I'd give it a shot. What did I have to lose? I could certainly use that!

But I wasn't at all prepared for what happened next.

It was as if I was zapped by a lightning bolt of God's love and power. Although I was standing far from the evangelist, it hit me without warning, knocked my feet out from under me, and sent me sprawling to the floor. I was embarrassed at first and tried to get up, but I couldn't. All I could do was lie there, as wave after wave of God's love and peace washed over, around, and through me.

Finally, with some assistance, I was able to get to my feet, but when I did, I staggered around like a drunken woman and then collapsed to the floor again!

I had never experienced such an exhilarating feeling in my life! No one had touched me, and I certainly wasn't prepared to collapse on the stage!

It wasn't until a month later that God revealed the full impact of what happened to me that night.

I was scheduled to undergo laser eye surgery to correct the increasing pressures on my optic nerve due to advanced glaucoma. When I went to see my ophthalmologist prior to the surgery, he came into his office shaking his head.

"What's wrong?" I asked.

"Wrong? There's nothing wrong," he said. "Nothing at all."

I didn't understand what he was saying at first.

"Lee," he said, "you don't need surgery. Your eyes are fine. After twelve years with glaucoma, it is gone and surgery is no longer necessary."

Even the astigmatism that had been with me all my life had disappeared! God had healed me, and I hadn't even realized it. And the reason I couldn't see well through my glasses was that my sight had been fully restored and I no longer needed the prescription lenses!

I hadn't asked for supernatural healing, hadn't expected it, and hadn't even recognized it when it came. But after that experience, I just naturally expected that God would do it again the next time I needed Him to dispense healing.

A BAD CASE OF THE FLU

It was the following January when Hal came down with what he thought was the flu. He felt nauseated, had no appetite, and was generally feeling weak and run down.

I remember asking him one day if he wanted me to fix him a sandwich.

"No," he said, waving me off. "I just don't feel like it." When he saw the worried look on my face, he tried to make a joke.

"At least I'm losing weight," he said, smiling. "And that's a good thing."

When "the flu" was still hanging on a month later, I insisted that Hal go to the doctor. And, because I wanted to make sure he told the doctor the truth about how he'd been feeling, I went with him.

The doctor didn't seem concerned.

"There's a lot of this going around," he said. "Just make sure you get plenty of rest, and you'll be fine."

Even though I practically demanded that he do so, he didn't see any reason to order any tests. This was an old-fashioned case of influenza—case closed.

(Would it surprise you if I told you that Hal and I belonged to an HMO medical insurance?)

Although it was against his nature, Hal tried to slow down and get as much rest as he could. It didn't help. Once or twice he thought he felt better for a day or two, but the queasy, weak feeling always came back.

Sunday was Mother's Day, and I was speaking at a church pastored by Hal's brother Don. It's a wonderful congregation of Bible-believing Christians in the Los Angeles Harbor area, and I was talking on the subject of using our faith to get through difficult situations.

I will never forget looking out into the congregation as I spoke that day and seeing how ill Hal looked. He was sitting next to his sainted mother, Nana, and I watched him sinking into the pew. I was almost afraid that he was going to wind up on the floor.

If this was the flu, it was more than stubborn.

Even so, when Monday came around, Hal still didn't want to go to the doctor.

"Look!" I half-shouted at him. "This thing has been hanging on for nearly four months, and you're not getting any better. You can hardly even walk! You're going to the doctor!"

For the first time, I saw what looked like fear in Hal's eyes. By this time I think he knew as well as I did that we were dealing with something more than the flu. Still, neither of us was prepared for, nor expected, what the tests were going to reveal.

Amazingly enough, the doctor still wasn't convinced that Hal needed any tests. He was sticking to his "give it time and it will pass" story, but I wasn't buying it.

"I'm not leaving your office until you give the order for a CAT scan," I told him.

"I really don't think that's nec——"

"Just look at him!" I shouted. "This is no flu! He needs help!"

When he saw that I wasn't going to give in, the doctor finally wrote the order and sent us for the scan.

31

Then we went home and waited for the phone call that would tell us what was really going on in Hal's body.

It didn't come until several hours later, and when it did, our doctor's voice sounded shaky over the telephone.

"Your liver is greatly enlarged, Hal," he said. "I'm afraid this is serious."

"What do you mean by serious?" Hal asked.

There was a momentary silence on the other end of the line. The doctor didn't want to say the words but had no choice.

"I'm afraid it's liver cancer," he said softly.

It embarrasses me now to think about how I acted. Listening in on an extension phone, I lit into him.

"How can you say it's cancer?" I asked. "Are you an oncologist? Do you treat cancer patients?" I hammered away at him, and I'm not really sure why. I guess I wanted him to say, "You know, you're right, it's probably not cancer after all." Maybe I figured that if I were mad enough, the cancer would get scared and go away.

"I can't believe you're telling us this over the phone!" I went on. "You can't know for sure."

The doctor seemed to understand my anger and agreed that further evaluation would be necessary. At the same time, he told us that he had set up an appointment with an oncologist for the following morning.

When we finally hung up the phone, Hal and I dissolved into tears in each other's arms.

How could this be happening to Hal, who was such a wonderful man? How could it be happening to us, who loved each other dearly and had committed our lives and our marriage to God's service? And yet, it *was* happening to us.

At that moment, we felt completely isolated and alone.

I knew even then that we weren't really alone, because God was with us.

INTO THE VALLEY OF THE SHADOW

The next day, the oncologist was all business. Very matter of fact. He could just as well have been talking about the weather. But he was talking about Hal's life.

He agreed with our doctor's prognosis that Hal was suffering from liver cancer, which had probably originated in his pancreas. As he talked in a matter-of-fact voice about the treatments that lay ahead, I found myself running through the entire list of "what ifs" that had formed in my mind.

What if Hal had gone to the doctor when he first felt sick?

What if I had insisted that the doctor run a series of tests right from the start instead of waiting for "the flu" to pass?

What if I had insisted that Hal get more rest and take better care of himself?

But no! I couldn't spend my time worrying about what had happened in the past. Hal and I both had to concentrate on the future, on overcoming this terrible disease and moving on with our life together.

The oncologist said that Hal would need to begin chemotherapy immediately. He talked about the possibility of shrinking the tumor, giving us hope that modern medicine could effect a cure. The truth was that Hal's cancer had progressed so far by the time it was diagnosed that there was very little hope at all, short of a supernatural miracle.

Had the oncologist been truthful with us, Hal and I probably would have decided together not to undergo the weeks of debilitating treatment.

Even though Hal and I did not understand totally the severity of his situation, we both knew that we had entered into a difficult, dangerous place the psalmist calls "the valley of the shadow of death."

As we read the Twenty-third Psalm together, we were reminded that David did not write, "Yea though I walk around the valley of the shadow of death," or "as I get too close for comfort to the valley of the shadow of death."

Rather, he wrote about walking "through" that terrible valley. And that's just what Hal and I were about to do.

SHIFTING GEARS

We decided that our first order of business had to be telling our family and friends about Hal's illness so they could help us pray Hal back to wellness. Neither Hal nor I were strangers to God's healing power. Both of us had seen God's love bring people back from the brink, and we both knew that the Book of James is right on target when it says, "The prayer of a righteous man is powerful and effective" (5:16).

Shortly after Hal's diagnosis, several trusted friends we knew to be "prayer warriors" gathered for a meeting in our home. It was a night of urgent, fervent prayer—the type of prayer that you just know is going to chase Satan and his soldiers all the way back to hell where they belong.

Before the evening was over, we were all in tears, but we were not crying due to despair over Hal's condition. Rather, they were tears of joy and hope over what God was about to do. Prophetic words of healing were even pronounced over Hal, and we felt certain that his healing would come soon.

I thought about how wonderful it would be to tell the doctor, "It looks like we won't be needing your chemotherapy after all. As you can see, God has healed Hal supernaturally!"

I half-expected Hal to feel better the next morning. Instead, he seemed to feel worse. And his doctors were saying we didn't have much time to lose. They wanted to start chemotherapy immediately.

Another meeting was called—this time a meeting of the Ezell family to discuss whether Hal should go ahead and start treatments.

Hal trusted the wisdom of his brother Don and his wife, Linda. Hal's mother was also there, along with our daughter Pam. Daughter Sandi, who lived two thousand miles away on the East Coast, joined us by telephone. As I looked around at their worried faces, I could see clearly how much they loved my husband—and me too. I knew they would be a source of strength and comfort to us both, no matter what God had planned for us, and I was right. Looking back, I don't know what either one of us would have done without their constant love and support.

Cancer is biological demon-possession; medical science is an attempt at exorcism.

There was a consensus that night that we should do what the doctors wanted us to do. After all, they were the experts, and we could all see that Hal seemed to be growing weaker and sicker day by day.

Since that night, I've come to an interesting realization about chemotherapy, and it's this: Cancer is biological demon-possession; medical science is an attempt at exorcism.

I remember the impression an old movie, *Fantastic Voyage,* made on me. Being a science fiction fan, I loved the film's premise of shrinking down a team of medical experts, placing them into a tiny, microscopic submarine, and injecting them into a patient's bloodstream. From there, they could sail around and attack the disease that was threatening the patient's life.

The only trouble was that the body's natural antibodies detected the submarine as an invader and began attacking it! Now, the patient in this movie had one strong immune system—something each of us needs to prevent cancer cells from growing within us.

How I wished I could find a minisubmarine full of cancer specialists who would be willing to take a fantastic voyage to the site of Hal's cancer! But that wasn't within the realm of possibility.

PLEASE, LORD, SHOW US WHAT TO DO!

Over the next few weeks, we were to learn a very devastating lesson—chemotherapy is awful stuff.

It involves flooding the body with poison. The hope is that you can kill the cancer without killing the body. Sometimes it does just the opposite.

Jackie Onassis suffered from lymphoma for years but was able to remain relatively healthy and active despite the disease. But then she checked into a hospital in New York and was dead three days later.

What happened? The doctors gave her a massive—and what later proved to be lethal—dose of chemo. The former First Lady did not die from lymphoma, but from acute poisoning from chemotherapy.[1]

After the first treatment, I wanted to yell "Stop!" But the oncologist assured me that all of the side effects were necessary if we hoped to halt Hal's cancer in its tracks. Still, it was hard to tell which had done more damage to my beloved husband—his illness or the means his oncologist was using to try to defeat that illness.

Meanwhile, friends from around the world were flooding us with surefire cancer cures, accompanied by plenty of testimonies to their effectiveness. There was a tea from the Orient, a serum from Germany, yams from South Africa, shark cartilage, cat's claw, and a number of other concoctions, foods, and potions that were just about guaranteed to conquer cancer. We even received an electromagnetic charging mechanism that was guaranteed to rid your body of cancer if you zapped yourself with it three times a day.

Some of these alternative methods of fighting cancer came wrapped in the news that there was a conspiracy to keep them from the general public. The American government, it was alleged, knew that a cure for cancer existed but was hiding it to protect the huge profits drug companies, hospitals, and doctors were making through chemotherapy and other standard treatments. I must admit, I was tempted to believe it. It would have been wonderful to know that a few electric shocks or a few plates of yams really would make Hal's cancer go away.

The confusion became even thicker when I logged on to the Internet to find the latest information on alternative cancer treatments. There were literally thousands of web pages devoted to the subject. Soon I was spending hours every day making phone calls and checking things out. It very easily could have become a full-time job.

It was not an easy matter to separate the out-and-out quackery from the alternative treatments that truly seemed to offer hope in the fight against cancer. Unfortunately, the people we talked to in the medical community quickly dismissed every alternative approach to cancer treatment as nonsense. Likewise, every holistic person we talked to told us to stay away from traditional cancer treatments. We were being pulled in opposing directions by two warring camps. There was no compromise at all.

"Please, God," we prayed, "show us what to do!" We didn't want to waste our time chasing after illusions or mirages. We wanted to know for sure that we were always moving in the right direction—toward a cure. I hoped that God would speak to me, saying something like, "Don't bother with those yams from South Africa, but that tea from the Orient is terrific." But He chose to remain silent. All we could do was pray that we were doing the right thing and then move ahead.

Looking back on what I learned during those days, I believe that anyone who is facing cancer should seek out the best of both traditional and holistic medicine. My hope is that someday, medical doctors and holistic practitioners will humble themselves, realize that they have some things to learn from each other, and start working together. When that day comes, I believe we will see real strides against all sorts of cure-resistant diseases, cancer among them.

37

As for Hal, he was always excited to hear about anything new I'd read or heard about. It gave him hope, and I was learning how very important hope can be to a person who is fighting for his life.

We also tried to maintain a positive attitude by posting reassuring signs around the house. These included Scriptures that lift the spirit, promises from God, funny sayings, loving greetings to each other, and so on. Hal also made two lists that we hung up. Each list had plenty of room for adding new items. The first list included a number of reasons why beating cancer was so important. It read like this:

Dreams to Live For
Our 25th anniversary (soon)
Our daughters' 40th birthdays
Our grandchildren's graduations
Nana's 90th birthday
Seeing Margaret remarry
Building a ministry to couples

The second list served to remind us that cancer *can* be beaten. It contained the names of several people who have won their battle against the disease and was labeled "Our Cancer Heroes." These included Emilie Barnes, Elaine Fleishman, Larry Burkett, Dave Dravecky, Betty Southard, John Ezell, Sue Buchanan, and Pat King.

I like what oncologist Sidney J. Winawer has to say about the importance of hope in his book, *Healing Lessons.* Dr. Winawer's perspective changed when his wife, Andrea, was diagnosed with cancer. When traditional treatments failed to help, she began looking into a number of alternative approaches, some of which were pretty far "out there."

Dr. Winawer would accompany his wife whenever she went to hear about some new treatment and writes that he would often be sitting there thinking, "This guy has no idea what he's talking about." But he always kept his negative reaction to himself because he didn't want to dim the hope that had begun to shine in his beloved wife's eyes. He wrote:

> Until Andrea's cancer, I had underestimated the value of hope. Now it tugged at me. If she could hope, I had to hope with her. I would lay aside my medical training, my instincts, my experience, as long as we could hope. . . . It seemed uncertain hope was better than hopeless certainty.[2]

LEARNING WHAT'S REALLY IMPORTANT

Another thing I was learning, besides the importance of hope, was how a diagnosis of cancer can change a person's perspective on life. Things that seemed urgent yesterday suddenly don't move you at all.

Frank Sinatra died the week of Hal's diagnosis. I had always been a huge fan, with a big stack of Old Blue Eyes' records. Under normal circumstances, his death would have caused me to stop, and perhaps even shed a tear or two. But now it was just another story on the evening news.

A friend who hadn't heard about Hal called me with what she thought was exciting information. She had discovered where we could buy retired Beanie Babies—CHEAP! She was so embarrassed when I told her what we were facing. But it was suddenly hard to believe that I had ever cared about Beanie Babies at all.

There was also a story on TV about another country trying to build up its nuclear arsenal. So . . . some renegade country just might blow up the world, huh? It was hard to care. It just didn't seem real. The only reality I knew was Hal, and I was determined to hang on to that wonderful reality for as long as I possibly could.

As the song says, the things of earth were becoming strangely dim.

🌿 ASKING . . . AND ACTING!

STEP 1: ASKING

Is your faith in God grounded in facts . . . or feelings? Why are facts more important than feelings?

STEP 2: ACTING

Make a list of facts that you know about God, then find at least one verse from God's Word to support that fact. Whenever you feel God is acting "out of character" in His dealings with you, go to your list and affirm what you know to be true about Him simply because "the Bible tells you so." I think it will help you trust Him, even when you can't figure Him out!

1. God is sovereign (Dan. 4:25).
2. God has loving plans for me (Jer. 29:11).
3.
4.
5.
6.

FOR BIBLE STUDY

Psalm 23
James 5:16

THREE

Looking for the Normal World

> He was despised and rejected by men,
> a man of sorrows, and familiar with suffering.
>
> Isaiah 53:3

Crazy!

That's what it was.

What in the world was I doing in the drugstore at this time of night?

What I appeared to be doing, to anyone who might be watching, was looking for a new shade of pink lipstick.

But what I was really doing, for a few minutes anyway, was trying to escape the daily battle with cancer. I was momentarily running away from my job as Hal's constant nursemaid, looking for a little bit of normalcy.

I wanted to feel like a woman again. Not a caregiver or a pill-distributor or a food-pusher, but just an ordinary gal.

And so when a friend dropped by to check on us, I asked her if she'd mind staying with Hal for a few minutes while I ran out to the drugstore. I didn't really need anything. I just had to get out of the house.

I should have known there was no such thing as escape. Even as I stood in front of that drugstore mirror, I was riddled with guilt over my "selfishness" at "deserting" Hal. What if he needed me? Question after question ran through my mind:

> *Had I given him all his medications?*
> *Had I watched his water intake so he wouldn't have to be getting up a lot during the night?*
> *Did I line up his "goodies" on his nightstand where he could reach them when he needed them?*
> *Could he reach his bell if he needed help?*

As I looked in that mirror, I discovered that my appearance was not exactly that of a "normal lady." My mascara was running down my cheeks. The creature staring back at me from that mirror looked more like a sad clown than a normal woman!

We were in the thick of the battle now.

Hal was getting chemotherapy on a daily basis, and as far as I could tell, it wasn't working.

His face was drawn and thin. His eyes were sunken. With every day that passed, he looked more like a victim of the Holocaust.

Meanwhile, our oncologist kept insisting that the treatments were helping.

I wasn't going to let that pass without a challenge, so we often clashed—always when Hal was out of the room. The situation was made worse by the fact that the doctor came from a Middle Eastern country where women are not encouraged to say what is on their minds. He obviously resented my questions.

"How can you tell me he's getting better?" I asked. "Just look at him!"

The doctor dismissed my concerns with a wave of his hand. "You're overreacting," he said. "You have to trust my judgment."

"I want to see the results of the latest blood work," I countered.

"You wouldn't understand it."

"I want to see it anyway."

And so it went.

We wanted to believe the doctor's report that the chemo was doing what it was supposed to do, but the deterioration in Hal was too swift and too obvious. In the days immediately following discovery of the cancer, Hal and I would take slow walks around the neighborhood. Very soon, he was using a walker. And then a wheelchair.

Looking back on what Hal and I went through, I can see four important principles for anyone dealing with cancer or a similar tragedy.

1. MAKE SURE YOU KNOW THE TRUTH

The Bible says the truth will "set you free," and it's true. If Hal and I had known the grim reality that we were facing, we might have spent the weeks and months of his illness in a different way. Only when you meet the reality of your situation head-on can you deal with it properly.

Even though we constantly asked for the truth, we didn't know that from the time Hal was first diagnosed with cancer, the honest prognosis was three months to live, with or without treatment. Again, had we known the truth, we almost certainly would have opted out of chemotherapy. Despite our doctors' assertions, the treatments Hal received did not do him one bit of good. Instead, they robbed us both of time that could have been spent together, enjoying each other's company.

I'm not blaming the doctor, really. Perhaps he was used to a strategy of keeping the truth from people who didn't really want to hear it. At the same time, I had stressed to him that neither Hal nor I were afraid of death, and that we wanted to know exactly what was going on.

As Hal's health deteriorated, I quickly became his primary, round-the-clock caregiver. Hal was up continuously during the night with pain, vomiting, or because he needed help to make it to the bathroom. It was mostly due to the naps he took during the day that he was able to get any sleep at all. I had no such luxury and began to lose weight.

Christian friends urged me to take sleeping pills or, at the very least, to drink a couple of glasses of wine before bed to help me sleep. But I refused. Early on, I had determined in my heart that I would not drug myself through this painful experience. I wanted to prove that God could get us through this terrible ordeal, just as He stood by Shadrach, Meshach, and Abednego when they were thrown into the fiery furnace.

I had no idea what sorrows would be ahead for me, but I didn't want to establish any bad habits in an attempt to ease the pain. As Bible scholar Eugene Peterson wisely observed, "Anesthesia, which is most useful on occasions of surgery, is most harmful in matters of the soul."

The majority of my concern was always for my beloved Hal, but the stress I was going through was intense. It wasn't just the long hours, the hard work, or the pain of seeing my husband in such a pathetic, weakened state and often in pain. All of those things were horrible, of course, but there were also tremendous financial pressures. Hal hadn't been able to work in many weeks, so he had no income.

When Hal was well, he could manage to juggle thirteen different projects and somehow stay on top of them all. But now, with Hal so sick that he couldn't even handle the tasks that came with day-to-day life, all of those projects were crashing. We could no longer maintain his car payments. (He couldn't drive anyway.) It looked very much

44

like we were going to have to close our office, which we'd been sharing for years. And there would be other cutbacks as well. We were down to the "you can't squeeze blood out of a turnip" stage.

Our financial situation dictated that I needed to accept every possible speaking engagement I could get. But even more than that, I needed to take care of Hal. So I started canceling most of my speaking engagements so I could stay at home with my honey.

Many of the people I called were immediately willing to let me bow out of the commitments I had made to them. They were sweet and kind and assured me that they would be praying for Hal and me. But others weren't so agreeable.

"You can't back out!" they said. "We've spent money on advertising! We've sold tickets! You have to come!"

When I protested that Hal needed me, I was told, "Listen, we had So-and-So come, and she was really sick, but she came anyway, and the Lord really blessed her. And we just know He'll do the same for you."

In such situations, I felt I had no choice but to pack my bags, often with tears in my eyes, and go off and try to encourage others while needing it myself. Believe me, it was not easy!

During those trips, Hal was never out of my thoughts and prayers for a moment:

Oh, Lord, here I am on the road again. I'm struggling to stay focused on ministering to folks while my heart remains back in California with my Hal. I feel split in half—my body here away from home, and my soul longing for healing for my West Coast husband. I'm grateful you dwell above time zones and distances. From your vantage point, you can take care of both of us at the same time, giving each of us what we need. As our hearts link in love, our souls

45

connect through the blood your Son shed for us. Care for us both tonight.

2. KEEP FIRST THINGS FIRST

When you're in the middle of a crisis, it's easy to get distracted by things that really aren't all that important.

Back home, the battle continued without a letup.

My one regret is that even when I was home with Hal, I was so busy. I spent hours on the Internet, trying to find some miracle cure. When I wasn't doing that, I was most likely fighting with our HMO, or taking care of other "urgent" matters.

I was reminded of all these frantic hours recently as I was writing a play about the biblical sisters Mary and Martha—a play my friend Pam Rozell and I have performed in many places. Of course, Pam plays the role of the sweet, devoted Mary, and I am the preoccupied, get-it-done Martha. (Talk about typecasting!)

This was never more true than when Hal was so ill. How I wish now I had taken Jesus' advice and chosen the "better part"—just to have sat and spent time with Hal, rather than being totally consumed with trying to find the answers to all our problems.

During this time, Hal wanted to do the things he had always done, but he just couldn't. Watching him become increasingly helpless broke my heart into little pieces.

On one occasion, as we walked out of the house on our way to the hospital for yet another round of treatment, Hal announced, "I'll drive." He proceeded to walk, on very unsteady feet, toward the driver's side of the car.

"Honey," I said, "you can't drive. You couldn't even pass a drunk driver's test!"

He smiled like a little boy who had just been "double-dog dared" to do something. "Oh yeah!" he said. "Then why don't you test me?" He wanted so much to be able to drive.

"Okay, I will!" I shot back.

I stood in front of him and said, "Touch your nose."

He did it, but just barely.

"Now walk a straight line up the driveway."

The first step wasn't too bad.

The second step was terrible.

He stumbled, I grabbed him to keep him from hurting himself, and we fell into each other's arms, laughing to keep from crying.

I had made my point. I would drive him to the hospital.

At night, after Hal fell asleep, I'd start plowing through all the paperwork, seeing what the insurance paid, what it didn't pay, and preparing to do battle over the treatments that should have been covered but weren't.

When I wasn't trying to reconcile hospital and doctor bills with insurance statements, I was filling out forms. State forms, federal forms, all kinds of forms—as I sought to obtain disability and social security benefits for my spouse.

Today, I proudly consider myself to be a VMW in good standing. That stands for Veteran of Medical Wars, and I have the battle scars to prove it!

3. As Much As Possible, Stay Positive

The Bible says, "Give thanks in all circumstances" (1 Thess. 5:18). Believe me, I know how hard this can be, but it's so important.

One night I became so frustrated with it all, I felt I couldn't take it anymore. I pushed my chair away from the table, stalked across the living room, and stared out the window for a few moments to capture my thoughts.

At that rather angry moment, I was suddenly reminded of what Jesus had done for me when He died on the cross.

"Lord," I said, "I'm grateful that Christ paid the premium for me to collect 100 percent of the peace of God! Even though I've never paid a penny into this plan, I know I'll reap the benefits for the rest of my life—and throughout all eternity!"

Thus encouraged, I also began to think about the fact that I lived in the United States, where at least there *were* benefits that I could apply for.

That calmed me down a bit, and I soon went back to the daunting pile of forms and papers in the middle of the table.

I must admit that I was grateful when our insurance company sent a social worker to evaluate our situation. He was someone "professional" to help me be sure I was giving Hal everything he needed.

As we were talking privately, he asked me, "Has your husband been sick a lot in his life?"

"No," I replied. "Hardly ever. Why?"

"Well," he explained, "that's good news and bad news. The bad news is that since he's not used to being sick, he's probably going to get pretty depressed. The good news is that if he can recover, he'll probably do it pretty fast. People who aren't used to being sick—who haven't made a lifestyle out of sickness—recover sooner. They don't want to be dependent."

Another vote, it seems, for positive thinking! Following the apostle Paul's advice, I began to seek out anything that was of good report.

4. KEEP YOUR EYES ON JESUS

Yes, there were times when Hal did get depressed. But most of the time he stayed up because he kept his mind on Jesus.

I would stand at the kitchen window and watch him out on the patio, worshiping the Lord with his hands uplifted in praise, singing along with a song he loved, "Sitting at the Feet of Jesus." He cherished that song, which Bill Gaither had arranged for his Homecoming Video Series, and Hal would ask me to play it over and over again, while he sang the words:

> Sitting at the feet of Jesus,
> There I love to weep and pray,
> While I from His fullness gather
> Grace and comfort everyday.

Although we were still trusting God for healing, it was apparent that Hal's body was wasting away. But his spirit? Oh, his spirit was growing stronger by the hour. He was Exhibit A for 2 Corinthians 4:16–17: "Though outwardly we are wasting away, yet inwardly we are being renewed day by day. For our light and momentary troubles are achieving for us an eternal glory that far outweighs them all."

Friend, whatever you may be going through, now is the time to find that God is with you, silently standing alongside.

He never left you or said, "I'll get back in touch with you when you're through this trial."

Why not reach out to touch Him with your faith right now? Feel the substance of the God-reality that you hope for. Now is the day of salvation for you.

Please don't miss out on interpreting what He means *now*, at this moment, all through the struggle. You must search for Him to appear each day, standing with you in the fiery furnace. It's time now to wash the smell of smoke from your garments and put on the garment of praise to fight off a heavy spirit. It works!

☘ASKING . . . AND ACTING!

STEP 1: ASKING

Do you really think it's possible to give thanks in all circumstances? Why or why not?

STEP 2: ACTING

Practice makes perfect! Fill in the blanks in the prayer of praise below, inserting the words that make it personal to your current struggles. Every morning this week pray this prayer . . . and keep on praying it until you mean it! Eventually I believe you'll see how praising God when it seems *unnatural* will lift you *supernaturally* above your circumstances. Here goes . . .

My heavenly Father,
I am hurting like crazy because _____
_____.
I don't understand why this is happening to me. It seems like You are treating me unfairly. I feel (list your emotions)_____. But I choose to praise You anyway, Lord. I don't want to, but I *choose* to. I love You because _____
_____. I trust You because _____. I praise You because You deserve it for what You've provided for me through Christ Jesus my Lord. Amen.

FOR BIBLE STUDY

Isaiah 53:3
2 Corinthians 4:16–17
1 Thessalonians 5:18

FOUR

When God Says No

*Redemption is not an exemption
from life's struggles.*

Why?

That was the question that haunted me as Hal continued his battle against cancer.

If God can heal all the sick people in the world with a simple snap of His fingers, then why doesn't He do it?

God moves in a *mischievous* way?

Sometimes it seems that way, doesn't it?

When Hal and I were trying to decide between chemotherapy and alternative treatments for his cancer, I didn't want to have to make a choice. I wanted God to intervene supernaturally so that Hal wouldn't need either kind of treatment.

After all, Hal and I both knew, beyond any doubt, that God is still the one "who heals all your diseases" (Ps. 103:3).

And that the Bible says, "The LORD brings death and makes alive; he brings down to the grave and raises up" (1 Sam. 2:6).

Thus it was, weeks later, that once we got over the initial shock and fear of Hal's diagnosis, I thought, *No problem. We'll just get him to a healing meeting.* After all, God had repaired my damaged eyes with one blast of healing power, and He certainly could—and would—do the same thing for Hal's liver and pancreas.

Hal's brother Don felt the same way. After all, as the pastor of a large Bible-believing church, Don had seen plenty of healings. So we bundled Hal in an airplane, and the two of them flew halfway across the country to a healing service where God's power was sure to be in action.

Yes! God was there! During the service, Hal felt God's touch! The loving warmth of the Lord's presence spread throughout his entire body. He just knew that he had been healed.

So did I.

We approached our oncologist and told him that we wanted another CAT scan.

The doctor, a devout Moslem, shook his head.

"It's too early to do that," he said. "You haven't been in treatment long enough. Another scan isn't going to tell us anything."

Hal and I both knew that scans are expensive—several thousand dollars. But we still wanted it done.

"I just know that Jesus has touched me," Hal told him. "I believe I've been healed."

The doctor shook his head again, sighed deeply, and signed the paperwork for us to get the scan done.

I will never forget sitting there, waiting for Hal to come out of that machine. There was going to be some kind of celebration in the Ezell house that night, let me tell you.

Then I saw the grim look on the face of the radiologist.

"I can't understand why your doctor ordered another scan so soon," he said. "I don't know what he was expecting to see, but your tumor has only grown larger."

I tried not to cry as I saw Hal's eyes filling up with tears. Talk about disappointment. Rejection. Humiliation. And yes, fear. All of those emotions were flooding through us as we left the hospital that day.

Hal still knew that he had been touched by God. But apparently it was not a healing touch. What a terrible blow to both of us!

Still, Hal never gave in to the grief and pain he was enduring, never stopped being a kind, considerate man—an example of strength and faith to everyone who knew him.

The Battle Continues

Not having received the healing he had expected, Hal continued to endure the debilitating effects of chemotherapy and other painful procedures.

Like paracentesis.

This particular time it was after midnight, and Hal and I were back in the emergency room at the hospital for this procedure.

There were two nurses in the room with us. One of them inserted a long needle into Hal's stomach. She was drawing out the excess fluid that had built up due to the cancer in his liver.

This was Hal's fourth time to go through paracentesis. The first two times, I was too much of a wimp to be present. I didn't want to see Hal suffer. And I was afraid I might get sick to my stomach. But I had finally come to the point where I had to be there, no matter what.

Hal needed me. To hold his hand. To wipe his brow. To tell him I loved him. And to pray silently that God would watch over us, protect us, and grant us the miracle of healing we still hoped for.

I closed my eyes and tried to remember what it felt like to have Hal's arms wrapped around me. Strong arms, squeezing me tight, letting me know how much he loved me, and that he never wanted to let me go. I didn't want to let him go either.

Neither one of us was afraid to die. But neither one of us was ready to say good-bye.

This wasn't our first visit to the hospital in the middle of the night. But it seemed different this time. There seemed to be a severe shortage of physicians, and everything had been left in the hands of people who wanted to help but didn't seem quite sure how to do it. Their perceived lack of confidence bothered me, but they were all we had.

When the procedure was finally finished, we were pushed into a room and told that "transportation" would be along soon to take Hal to the Intensive Care Unit.

Five minutes passed, and there was no sign of transportation.

Ten minutes.

Fifteen.

As his blood pressure plummeted, I finally decided we had waited long enough. My husband's life was hanging in the balance, and I wasn't going to stand there and watch him die.

I summoned the few faithful friends who had accompanied us to the hospital. We disconnected a wire here, another one over there, and we were soon pushing Hal and his gurney down the hall toward the ICU.

The crew saw us coming and hurried to meet us. They took over immediately and began hooking Hal up to a series of monitors and gauges that hummed, whirred, and clicked as they went about their business of measuring whatever amount of life was left in Hal's physical body.

After a long while, the nurse in charge came over, put her hand on my shoulder, and told me that I ought to go home and get some rest.

"But do you really think . . . ?" I protested.

"I know how you feel," she said sympathetically. "But your husband has been stabilized, and he's sleeping comfortably."

I felt a flush of embarrassment, because I knew she was staring at the dark circles under my eyes.

"You've got to get some rest," she said. "You owe it to yourself . . . and to your husband."

She was right. How was I going to take care of Hal if I let my own health deteriorate?

I didn't want to leave, but I was desperate for a few hours of sleep.

I felt better about going home when our faithful friend Margaret told me she would stay and "keep watch" over Hal. Margaret had lost her own husband in this same hospital so she, more than anyone else, knew what I was going through.

I know I prayed on the way home, but I'm not sure what I said. Whatever it was, it wasn't eloquent. You don't make pretty speeches when you're screaming for someone to throw you a life preserver to save you from drowning.

I had just inserted my key into the lock of my front door when I heard the phone ringing inside. Frantically, I pushed the door open, ran across the darkened living room, and grabbed the phone.

"Hello?" I gasped, hoping it would be a wrong number. Otherwise, it couldn't be good news. Not at 1 A.M.

Instead, it was Margaret.

"Lee," she said, "Hal's taken a turn for the worst. They've called a code blue. Hurry."

I didn't know what code blue meant, but I knew it was bad.

I slammed the phone down, raced to the car, and sped back to the hospital as tears streamed down my face.

When the elevator doors opened onto the eighth floor, and I saw Margaret's ashen face in front of me, I knew what had happened.

Her words confirmed it.

"He's gone!" she blurted out. "I'm sorry, but Hal's gone!"

I felt at that moment that the world had suddenly stopped turning. And then I went numb.

Hal was dead.

I didn't even get to tell him good-bye.

I found out later that the paracentesis had punctured Hal's stomach and caused internal bleeding, which was not discovered until it was too late. If a doctor had been on hand that night to make sure the procedure was done properly . . .

But that's not fair! Hal had been dying a little more every day. That was obvious. If death hadn't stolen him away from me on that tragic night, it would have come for him soon enough.

I never thought the paracentesis was responsible for Hal's death anyway. There was plenty of blame to go around.

- Blame for the cancer that had struck without warning.
- Blame for the treatments that often seemed to do more harm than good.
- Blame for some in the medical community who never told us the truth about Hal's condition.
- Blame for myself, for failing to be there when the end came.
- And blame for God, Who chose not to heal Hal.

PICKING UP THE PIECES

I didn't want to blame God, of course. But my mind was full of difficult, painful questions.

Doesn't God's Word tell us that all things work together for good for those who love Him?

But what possible good could come out of this wonderful man's death?

How could it be good that I had been left alone to pick up the pieces of my life—which seemed scattered all around me, like so many shards of broken glass, waiting to be swept up and tossed into the trash?

I turned to the Book of James.

Yes, it was still in there:

> Is any one of you sick? He should call the elders of the church to pray over him and anoint him with oil in the name of the Lord. And the prayer offered in faith will make the sick person well; the Lord will raise him up.
>
> James 5:14–15

Why hadn't that worked for my Hal?

I would have to begin a new chapter in understanding God's mysterious ways.

I had to remind myself that the apostle Paul struggled too. That's why he wrote these words:

> We are hard pressed on every side, but not crushed; perplexed, but not in despair; persecuted, but not abandoned; struck down, but not destroyed.
>
> Therefore, do not lose heart. Though outwardly we are wasting away, yet inwardly we are being renewed day by day. For our light and momentary troubles are achieving for us an eternal glory that far outweighs them all. So we fix our eyes not on what is seen, but on what is unseen. For what is seen is temporary, but what is unseen is eternal.
>
> 2 Corinthians 4:8–9, 16–18

 ASKING . . . AND ACTING!

STEP 1: ASKING

When God says no, do you feel He is:

Punishing you?
Protecting you from something worse?
Teaching you something?
Helping you grow?

Have you ever said no to anyone for any of the above reasons?

STEP 2: ACTING

Okay. So this is not such a new idea, but it's a good one anyway! Next time you feel God has been unfair to you, take a piece of paper and draw a vertical line down the center. Label the left side "Yes" and the right side "No." Make two lists, one for the times when God answered your prayers affirmatively and another for the times when He gave you a thumbs-down. Which list is longer?

FOR BIBLE STUDY

1 Samuel 2:6
Psalm 103:3
2 Corinthians 4:8–9, 16–18
James 5:14–15

FAITH . . . OR PRESUMPTION?

In this world, you will have trouble.

John 16:33

Friends.

You never know who they are until you need them. And you never know which ones will be there to minister God's love to you in times of trouble.

When Hal got sick, I was surprised and delighted to discover that we had dozens of friends.

They wrote. They called. They stopped by. They let us know they were praying, and that they expected Hal to get well.

But then a funny thing happened to some of them. When Hal didn't get well, they disappeared!

Not that I really blame them.

Well, at least I'm trying not to blame them.

They just didn't know what to do or how to handle the situation, so they stayed away. Not everybody, of course. Many of our good friends hung in with us all the way to the end.

But there were those who departed, seemingly because Hal did not live up to their expectations. They had prayed for him and they expected him to get well. It really was that simple.

I was hoping for a word of wisdom but got only words of wishful thinking.

When he didn't jump out of his sick bed with enough supernatural energy and strength to run in a Boston Marathon, they turned away. To this day, I don't know whether they were disappointed in Hal and me, or whether they had to turn their backs on us because their "faith in faith" couldn't withstand a collision with the brutal reality of Hal's terminal illness.

In the early stages of Hal's fight with cancer, many confident believers gave us "words from the Lord." They used Scripture and prophetic words to assure us that Hal would not die. I wanted to believe—and for a while did believe—that the encouraging messages they delivered came from God Himself. I know now that they came, instead, from the hearts of sincere Christians who wanted to see Hal made whole, but who had no reassurance from God that this was going to happen. Looking back on it now, I realize that I was hoping for a word of wisdom but got only words of wishful thinking.

During the course of Hal's illness, some of these people would call or stop by to get the latest "positive report" on Hal's condition. They wanted to hear that the tumor was shrinking, that his energy was returning, that things were looking great! Oh, how I wanted to tell them what they wanted to hear, but I couldn't. The truth was the tumor was growing, Hal's energy was waning, and I was demoralized and discouraged, even as I struggled to understand God's purposes and hang on to His hand.

When I couldn't give them the news they wanted, they eventually disappeared, leaving me feeling abandoned. Actually, betrayed would be a better word, and praying a prayer like this:

Remember me, Lord? I'm one of your kids who believes in healing. Count me among those extremists who believe in receiving the Master's touch. I'm even one of those who has experienced divine healing by Your hand. I'm not a doubter. You don't have to show me the nail prints in Your hand. I know You suffered in our place. The punishment for our peace was laid upon You, so that by Your stripes we can be healed.

But in spite of all my believing, I don't see things improving. I've stood fast, laid hold, and loosed it at the same time. What a divine paradox! I've named it and claimed it. I've nabbed it and grabbed at it, but healing still eludes us. It all seems to be wound around timing and Your sovereignty, neither of which I can affect or persuade. Again, I must admit power-lessness—even in the face of having all things in Christ. Again, I'm thrown prostrate on Your mercy.

Why didn't God choose to heal Hal? I don't know.

Why does any good person ever have to suffer? I don't know the answer to that question either.

But after many days and nights spent in agony, wrestling with God and looking for answers, I have come to a few important conclusions:

1. It is very easy to confuse faith with presumption.
2. God is sovereign and always has His purposes.
3. Anyone who thinks Christians shouldn't have to suffer isn't reading the same Bible I'm reading.
4. Prayer does work!

CONFUSING PRESUMPTION WITH FAITH

First, I want to talk about the difference between faith and presumption.

David wrote, "Keep back thy servant also from presumptuous sins" (Ps. 19:13).

Some Christians act as if God is some sort of fairy godfather who only wants us to be happy, healthy, and prosperous. When Hal was sick, these people told me the formula was simple: "Believe it . . . say it . . . and then receive it."

*My desires were writing checks
that my faith couldn't cash.*

The problem is that this belief system takes the future out of God's hands and puts the responsibility on us. If we believe enough, pray enough, and quote enough Scripture, everything will be fine.

When Hal died, our dear family and friends who were revved up to be assured that "the devil will not take Hal's life" were overwhelmed by guilt and confusion. We did everything according to the Book, and it didn't work. When Hal's health was deteriorating, I felt like a faithless failure because I couldn't seem to do anything about it. My desires were writing checks that my faith couldn't cash.

Since then, I've learned that real faith does not rise from a pep talk—or a faith pep rally. And I've learned that I have some pretty impressive company when it comes to my inability to always get God to do what I want Him to do.

Consider the apostle Paul's "thorn in the flesh." The Bible doesn't tell us what this "thorn" was. But in the twelfth chapter of 2 Corinthians, Paul says that he prayed three times for the Lord to take it away and that God did not grant his prayer. Does this mean Paul was lacking in the faith department?

Hardly!

Here was a man who was so full of faith that "even handkerchiefs and aprons that had touched him were taken to the sick, and their illnesses were cured" (Acts 19:12). If anybody knew God's healing power, it was Paul. And yet he apparently spent his entire life suffering from his "thorn in the flesh." Furthermore, it apparently did not hurt Paul's faith one iota that God refused to supernaturally heal him.

Three other situations from the life of Paul also come to mind.

The first, his admonition to his young friend Timothy to "stop drinking only water, and use a little wine because of your stomach and your frequent illnesses" (1 Tim. 5:23). The apostle never derided Timothy for being a weak, ill Christian. He never said, "You know, if you had enough faith, you'd stop being sick all the time." He didn't even say, "Next time I'm in town, I'll heal that problem for you."

The second situation has to do with a man named Trophimus. We don't know much about him, except that he accompanied Paul on one of his missionary journeys. In his second letter to Timothy, the apostle says, "I left Trophimus sick in Miletus" (2 Tim. 4:20). What, Paul? You mean you didn't have enough faith to heal him?

And finally, there's Epaphroditus. In the second chapter of Philippians, Paul writes that this fellow "was ill, and almost died. But God had mercy on him, and not on him only but also on me, to spare me sorrow upon sorrow" (v. 27).

Can't you just hear the message Paul is trying to lay between the lines? "Listen, this guy's not in good health, and frankly, it worries me. I don't want to be the cause of his death, so I'm sending him home where he can take it easy for a while."

Paul, why didn't you just lay hands on him and heal him?

Because Paul understood that there is a difference between faith in God and faith in faith. When I read the story of Paul, as recorded in the Book of Acts, I see that God expects us to go on serving Him and believing in Him *in spite of* the troubles that might come our way and not because He has delivered us out of them all.

As Barbara Brown Taylor writes:

> God . . . is not in the business of granting wishes. There is nothing wrong with letting God know what we want, as long as we do not mistake our list of wishes for the Covenant. The Covenant is no deal.[1]

In other words, God is not a cosmic errand boy who comes running whenever we beckon. Man was created to serve God and not the other way around! Anyone who believes that God is always going to give her whatever she wants whenever she wants it has gone beyond faith into presumption. I've discovered that true faith is hanging on to God no matter what's going on in your life.

When I first decided I needed to write this book, I traveled to the CBA (Christian Booksellers Association) annual convention to visit with a number of publishers. My goal was to find the publisher that best understood and appreciated my message and wanted to help me get it "out there," into the hands of suffering people who need to hear it.

A friend had recommended a small publishing house, so I decided to pop by their booth and tell them what I had in mind. I hadn't gone very far when the woman I was talking to held up her hand to stop me.

"At this publishing house, we believe in divine healing," she said, with an icy haughtiness in her voice. "We believe God takes care of His people." Then she launched into a well-rehearsed sermon on faith. As she talked, my eyes scanned the covers of the company's new releases. All the titles had to do with living in victory and prosperity. Things like *Victory Over Illness* and *God Wants You to Prosper,* and so on.

I interrupted to ask who owned the publishing house she represented, and she responded with a name I recognized.

"I'd love to see him again," I said. "Is he here?"

"Oh, no," she answered. "He went home to be with Jesus last year."

"Oh, I hadn't heard that," I said sympathetically. "What happened?"

"Cancer," she said softly.

I didn't want to be rude. But then again, I couldn't help myself.

"But didn't that cause you to reevaluate . . . ?"

She knew where I was going, and she didn't want to wait until I got there.

"Absolutely not!" she shot back. "God's Word is true, and it says that God never takes life, He only gives it! There are only two places where the Word says, 'God took him.' [I think she was referring to Enoch and Elijah.] Everyone else *chooses* to give up the ghost."

"And did the owner of your company . . . ?"

"Absolutely. He told his wife that he would be gone by morning and pointed to heaven. It was his choice to go."

I was really ticked off (in a righteous way, of course). I closed up my material, along with the few items she gave me to "help my understanding" and walked away. Her materials went straight into the nearest trash can. The hard, uncompassionate spirit she exhibited spoke volumes more than her doctrinal stand.

How it must frustrate God to see the way we twist the Scriptures, choosing what we want to accept and believe and ignoring everything that seems to conflict with our prejudiced viewpoint.

I certainly do not mean to climb up on my soapbox here, or to start preaching. That's not my style. My purpose is to encourage people and lift them up. But there are some things I just can't ignore. And one of those is this out-of-context faith doctrine that is causing so much harm to so many suffering Christians today!

"Faith people" reason something like this:

- Disease and suffering came into the world as a result of the curse placed on Adam and Eve.
- Jesus came to free us from the curse.
- Consequently, Christians should not be sick or suffer.

But there was more to the curse than sickness and pain.

For example, God told Adam that part of the curse was that he would have to work hard to make a living. If that portion of the curse no longer applies to us, then why do any of us have to work? Why doesn't God just supernaturally give us all the money we need?

God said that for women, part of the curse would be the pain of childbirth. I know from personal experience that giving birth is no walk in the park. Why not? If that portion of the curse were lifted, having a baby would be great fun, wouldn't it?

Consider a man who goes to an evangelistic meeting with a cold and ends up accepting Christ. If he still has the cold, does that mean he has not truly been converted? Of course not! That man received "the whole package" when he came to Christ, but physical healing is not always necessarily a part of that package. Now he's a Christian with a cold.

Picture two Christians seated side by side in church. One is feeling on top of the world while the other is in deep emotional pain. Both are equally worthy of God's blessing. Then why does one suffer while the other goes through life unscathed? The suffering brother feels that he has done something wrong. Feelings of guilt are oozing out of every pore. Has he demonstrated a lack of faith? Is he further away from God than the other fellow? This man's faith can too easily be sabotaged when life is unfair to him. The purveyors of the "prosperity gospel" would have us believe this is true, but life and the Bible simply don't back it up.

The eleventh chapter of Hebrews talks about some of the great heroes of faith. What happened to them? Some were tortured, others were whipped or torn apart, still others were stoned or killed with the sword.

Let's remind ourselves that God does not work for us. We work for Him!

What was the matter with these dudes? Didn't they believe in health and prosperity? And why didn't God step in and prevent all these calamities?

If I were the only one who had wrestled through this faith thing and lost, I wouldn't bother sticking my neck out about it. But I've talked with literally hundreds of people who lost the battle and are now casualties of war. These wounded warriors wind up confused, hurt, and wondering what went wrong. Many of them have been taught to believe that if they remind God often enough of His promises, they'll get what they want from Him.

Once in a stage production of *Fiddler on the Roof*, I had the opportunity to play Golda, the mama. All through the rehearsals, I would hear Reb Tevye (the old father) stop, look up toward heaven, and try to quote a Scripture to God. Over and over, he would remind God, "As the good Book says . . ." and then would quote one of the Bible's promises. Toward the end of the play, he says again, "As the good Book says . . ." Then he stops in midsentence, chuckles, and says, "But why should I tell *You* what the good Book says?" Let's remind ourselves that God does not work for us. *We* work for Him!

GOD IS SOVEREIGN AND ALWAYS HAS HIS PURPOSES

Does God perform miracles? You bet He does! Does He heal supernaturally? Yes!

But it's important to remember that God is in charge of this universe, not us. After all, He's the Creator, we're the created, and although we can be sure that He always acts with perfect love, we can never know for certain what form that love will take!

God deals with every person and every situation on an individual basis. It would not be fair of me to demand of you that your relationship with God be just like mine, or that He deal with you exactly as He has dealt with me.

An acquaintance had an inoperable brain tumor. He wrote down the Scripture from Isaiah 53, "with his stripes we are healed" (KJV), and pasted it on his bathroom mirror. Then, every morning when he shaved, he read those words and, through faith, applied them directly to his illness. Today, twenty years later, he is well and healthy.

Why didn't that kind of approach work for Hal? I don't know. I just know that God is sovereign, that I trust Him, and that I believe He will give me the answers to all my hard questions someday!

Meanwhile, I believe that the extreme emphasis from the "I am in charge, by the power of my faith" attitude has caused tremendous wreckage in the body of Christ. The pathway is strewn with "wounded warriors" who fought the battle valiantly and lost. The bankruptcy could not be stopped . . . the disease could not be arrested . . . the child was not born perfect.

All of these are catastrophic events. But well-meaning Christians who point fingers and say, "What happened to you?" can make things worse. "Just didn't have enough faith to beat this thing, huh?"

Some in the crowd at the crucifixion taunted Christ for His lack of faith. They said, "He saved others . . . but he can't save himself" (Matt. 27:42). How ironic! They didn't know that He was saving the whole world! There was a very important purpose for His suffering.

Remember this when you feel you are suffering for no good reason and some look at you as if to say: "If you're so spiritual, why can't you get what you're praying for?"

During the time when I was praying so fervently for Hal's healing, I read the story of Shadrach, Meshach, and Abednego from the third chapter of Daniel. I'm sure you know the story. The three devout men refused to worship the idol that King Nebuchadnezzar had set up, and so they were thrown into a fiery furnace. God delivered them from that trial by fire, and when they came out of the furnace, the Bible says "their robes were not scorched, and there was no smell of fire on them" (v. 27). They didn't even smell like smokers!

But what I noticed, when I read the story for the umpteenth time, was that Shadrach and his friends didn't feel that there was any guarantee God would rescue them. When the king threatened to throw them into the furnace, they said, "If we are thrown into the blazing furnace, the God we serve is able to save us from it. . . . But even if he does not, we want you to know, O king, that we will not serve your gods or worship the image of gold you have set up" (Dan. 3:17–18).

They did not haughtily pronounce, "Go ahead, try to throw us in, we dare you! Our God won't allow it!" Instead, they humbly trusted themselves to God's care.

Now, that's faith!

They were saying, in effect, "Our God is sovereign, and we know He can rescue us if He chooses to do so. But even if it costs us our lives, we're still not going to worship the idol you've set up."

God, give me faith like that!

CHRISTIANS WILL SUFFER

Anyone who believes Christians won't have to suffer must not be reading the same Bible I'm reading. The Bible is full of examples of people who grew to a new level of faith and closeness to God *through* suffering—Joseph, Jeremiah, Stephen, to name just a few.

As Hal and I were dealing with his illness, we actually took great comfort from those Scriptures that talked about suffering. They reminded us that we were not alone in our trials, that God was with us in the midst of them, and that He weeps right along with us when we are in pain.

I'm not going to take the time to quote all the many Scriptures that have to do with suffering. But if anyone tells you that a peaceful, pain-free life is the mark of a Christian, tell them to take another look at Hebrews 11, the Book of James, and 1 Peter. You might also suggest that they read through the Book of Acts and rediscover all the difficult times the apostle Paul went through.

You know the old saying that misery loves company? Well, when you and I suffer, we've got plenty of company!

No, I do not believe that it's God's will for people to suffer. Our afflictions are not predestined. I am not like the pessimistic Christian who fell down the stairs and immediately said, "Thank God that one's over with!" But neither do I believe it is His will that we should sail through life unscathed and untouched by tragedy and trouble. Tragedy and trouble, after all, are the means through which we grow and become more like Christ.

I do not expect a storm, but I have prepared my spiritual storm shelter, just in case. In this way, I insure against spiritual devastation should I be caught in another emotional catastrophe.

Because I live in California, I may have a better understanding of this than people who live in other states. I am not expecting "the big one," as some call the devastating earthquake that is supposed to happen here "someday." But even though I don't expect it, in my garage I've got an earthquake box full of things I'll need in an emergency. (I also keep a pair of shoes under my bed and a flashlight within reach—just in case.)

I've come to two conclusions about pain and trouble:

1. They are a part of life on this planet and have been ever since Adam and Eve took a big bite out of the forbidden fruit and let sin into the Garden of Eden.
2. When I look at news reports from around the world regarding the persecution Christians are enduring, I realize that Christians often suffer *more* than nonbelievers do—not less!

The plain truth is, suffering happens. But some Christians act like cartoon character Charlie Brown, who said he believed that no problem was so big or so important that it couldn't be run from. We think that maybe if we pretend it isn't there, trouble will just go away and leave us alone.

That's what I call "sanctified denial," and it doesn't work. If that's how we Christians act, then we may as well be Christian Scientists, who deny everything. Success isn't happening. Evil isn't happening. It's all an illusion. No, one of the great things about Christianity is that it gives us the ability to stare evil, suffering, and death right in the face and say, "Where is your sting?"

And even though God may not automatically intervene in our circumstances, I believe with all my heart that He will redeem them.

Pastor James Van Tholen, coming back to give his first sermon after prolonged cancer treatment, said:

We can't ignore what has happened. We can rise above it; we can live through it; but we can't ignore it. If we ignore the threat of death as too terrible to talk about, then the threat wins. Then we are overwhelmed by it, and our faith doesn't apply to it. If that happens, we will lose hope.[2]

PRAYER WORKS

Have I given up on prayer? Not at all. I know that prayer works. Even in the midst of Hal's suffering, prayer was a means of drawing close to God. I believe that God did touch Hal during that service, but it was not a healing touch. It was a touch that said, "I love you and I am with you always . . . even unto the end."

I continue to pray conscientiously. I expect to see miraculous answers to my prayers. But I have learned to leave things in God's hands, trusting that even if He does not give me what I ask for or want, He will give what is best.

The fifth chapter of John tells the story of the Pool of Bethesda. The Bible says that an angel stirred up the waters of this pool every now and then, and when that happened, the first one into the water was healed. Well, whenever I sense that God is stirring my waters, I'm going to try my best to be the first one in the pool. Yes, I still believe in prayer! Yes, I still believe in healing!

Some feel it's safer not to mix faith with tragic situations, that it's too risky. They think that perhaps God will come through, and then again, maybe He won't. They try to hedge their bets, and if God does show up, so much the better. What a godless attitude!

Do I regret handling Hal's illness with positive faith? No! The regrettable thing is the tease—the illusive promise that "according to your faith you will receive." I feel cheated mostly, and it all came back to me when I heard author and speaker Jim Conway, who lost his dear wife, Sally, to cancer.

In a speech he gave at the Crystal Cathedral, he talked about the last nine months of her life, which she spent in her bed at home. He talked about how beautiful those last weeks were, as all the family talked together about heaven, and Sally's being called home soon. Sally laid hands on each family member, blessing them, and expressing her wishes for them all. They sang hymns together. She went

72

out in a blaze of glory. Nothing was left unsaid. No loose ends were left dangling. How I wish it would have been like that for Hal.

Still, there were wonderful moments, gifts from God sprinkled here and there.

I will never forget the day God lifted our spirits in His unique way. As I sat in the hospital lobby, reading a magazine and waiting for Hal's doctor to perform another one of dozens of "procedures," I looked up into the face of Oral Roberts.

His wife, Evelyn, was with him.

"Now, isn't this the lady we saw on television, Evelyn?" he asked. "You were using humor to preach the gospel, right?" I stood to my feet and greeted them both, and they were warm and approachable.

Evelyn explained that her husband had been complaining of some discomfort and she had brought him in for an X ray. They wanted to know what I was doing there, but before I could finish telling them, the nurse came and led us back to the ward, where Dr. Roberts had been assigned the bed right next to Hal!

I asked Dr. and Mrs. Roberts if they would wait out in the hall just a minute while I announced to Hal, "Guess who I found in the hallway?"

You should have seen Hal's jaw drop open as Oral Roberts walked toward his bed with hand outstretched, saying, "Well, bless you now, Brother Ezell."

Then, Mrs. Roberts stepped forward and began preaching a minisermon. "Now, Brother Ezell," she said, "you have made a lot of deposits in your heavenly bank account. Have you told the Lord you want to make a withdrawal today for this successful procedure?"

Hal mumbled something back in his shock, and she continued to exhort him.

"God," I silently prayed, "thank You for this."

Asking . . . and Acting!

STEP 1: ASKING

If God had not created night and day, would you have ever seen a sunrise? Do our "dark nights of the soul" make our faith a beautiful treasure?

STEP 2: ACTING

I don't know about you, but *music* gives me a lift. Why not stop what you are doing right now and put on your favorite CD or tape. Lie down on the sofa, close your eyes, and let the music lift you above your grief and pain. Hum along or, better yet, belt it out at the top of your lungs! You'll feel better, and God will really enjoy having you sing a concert, just for Him.

FOR BIBLE STUDY

Psalm 19:13	2 Corinthians 12
Isaiah 53	1 Timothy 5:23
Daniel 3:17–18, 27	2 Timothy 4:20
Matthew 27:42	Hebrews 11
John 5; 16:33	James
Acts 19:12	1 Peter

SIX

GRACE AT DEATH'S DOOR

*The beauty of a well-lived life becomes a legacy that stays
behind and warms the heart recalling every memory.*

Tears.

There were plenty of those in the last days of Hal's life.

And even more in the days immediately following his
death.

But there was laughter too. It came at unexpected moments, breaking through the gloom and reminding us that
there are many good things in life that remain constant,
even in a time of incredible suffering and sorrow.

Things like children—and friends.

All I can say about children is "thank God" for them,
for their innocence and trust. No wonder Jesus said that anyone who wants to enter the kingdom of heaven must
become like a little child.

Shortly after Hal passed away, my six-year-old grandson,
Mason, visiting with his family from the East Coast, insisted
that he wanted to sleep with me "on Papa's side" of the bed

so I wouldn't get lonely. He wiggled and squirmed all night long, but that was all right. He kept me from being lonely.

The next morning, he told me he wanted to take me out for pancakes. In my numb state, I complied, telling everyone else we'd be back shortly.

I didn't know that he wanted to get me alone because he had a plan.

"Now GiGi, Papa is in heaven, right?"

"Right."

"And he's not coming back, right?"

"Right."

"Then you have to get a new husband," he advised, holding his hands up in a gesture that said, "That should be obvious."

"Oh no, Mason," I said. "I don't want another husband. I was happy with Papa."

He wasn't going to take no for an answer. "Then why not get another one that *looks* like Papa?" he asked.

He had me laughing by then.

"But Mason," I said, "I don't know how to find another husband. What would I do?

"It's simple!" he sighed, exasperated by my ignorance. "You just put gas in your van. Then you drive around until you're out of gas. The first man you see then, you say, 'Would you like to be my husband?' If he says no, then get more gas, get back in your van, and drive around again!"

There you have it! Wonderful advice to anyone who may be looking for a mate. Straight from the heart of a six-year-old. How could my single friends have missed this simple solution for so long?

And then there were so many wonderful friends who surrounded us with their love. They stayed with us all the way through Hal's illness and comforted me in the days after he went to heaven.

I owe such a debt of gratitude to friends like Margaret Harvey. The Ezell and Harvey families have been close for more than twenty years. After Margaret's husband, Jon, died of cancer, she began traveling with me around the country, acting as my personal assistant.

Another one of Hal's good friends, Ryan, flew all the way from Johannesburg, South Africa, to spend a few hours with us. He spent lots of money and many hours in the air, just so he could pray with Hal and let him know how much he loved him.

Two little boys from our neighborhood, Chad and Troy MacDonald, wanted to give Mr. Ezell something special, so they sent him one of their precious Beanie Babies—the All-American Glory bear—to cheer him up. Believe me, it was special to Hal because he knew how much the sacrifice meant to those little boys.

Other touching gifts and notes arrived on an almost daily basis. Hal received many light-hearted cards which lined our fireplace mantel. One of these contained a joke that gave Hal a much-needed belly laugh:

> A hospitalized husband weakly motioned for his wife to come near. As she leaned over he whispered, eyes full of tears, "My dear, you have been with me all through the bad times. When I had the car wreck, you were there. When my business failed, even when we lost the house, you were always there. Do you know what?"
>
> Smiling, she replied, "What dear?"
>
> He answered, "I think you're bad luck!"

My daughter, Julie (of *The Missing Piece* book), has two teenage children who made cards for their grandfather. Thirteen-year-old Casey sent him an invitation to her future wedding, because she didn't want him to miss out on the big day, whenever it comes. Her eleven-year-old brother, Herb, sent his grandfather an invitation to his 2006 high school graduation, complete with a doctored up picture of himself in a cap and gown.

Those cards were such a treasure to Hal.

MAKING PREPARATIONS FOR THE END

I will never forget the kindness of our dear friend Clyde Martin, who flew in from northern California and helped us make some preparations for Hal's departure.

Clyde was Hal's oldest and dearest friend, and as such, he was able to talk to Hal about preparing for the eventuality of death in a way that I never could have done.

"Listen, Hal," he said, "I'm not here because I think you're about to die. I just want to make sure you've taken care of things so that when the time comes, you're ready."

He pulled out a microcassette tape recorder. "For instance, does Lee know what kind of funeral you want?"

"Of course she does," Hal replied.

I shook my head, "No, I don't. I suppose you want your funeral at your brother's church, but that's about all I know."

Now it was Hal's turn to shake his head. "No," he said, "I want my funeral at the Crystal Cathedral. Nothing ostentatious, but I definitely prefer the Cathedral."

"Yes," I said, laughing, "and I'd like to be crowned Miss America, but it's not going to happen. Get serious. Tell me what you really want."

"I am serious," he replied. "You asked me what I wanted and I told you."

I rolled my eyes at what I considered to be a rather unusual and unrealistic request, but Clyde just kept the tape rolling.

"And who would you like to speak at the service."

"Well, I'd like my brother to be in charge," Hal began, "but I'd also like Loren Cunningham to speak."

"Oh, Hal," I protested. "Now you really are being unreasonable. You know how impossible Loren's schedule is." Loren Cunningham had been Hal's friend since childhood, when they had met at a church camp. But he had gone on to found the world's largest international part-time missions program, Youth With a Mission. Loren is always hidden away in some secret jungle of the world, opening doors for the spreading of the gospel. Expecting him to return to the States for Hal's funeral would really be expecting too much.

"But I'd really like him to speak," Hal said again, and rather than frustrate him, I dropped the subject.

Clyde gently went on to ask Hal about the music he wanted and a myriad of other questions that I never could have brought myself to ask, even though they were important ones. I couldn't ask them because it would have been like saying, "Hal, we both know you're going to die, and we might as well admit it." But Clyde had a way that was forceful and gentle at the same time. How I appreciated his stepping in and taking charge the way he did.

"So now, Hal," Clyde said as he turned off the tape, "don't you feel better knowing that Lee knows what you want? We'll just put this tape in your safe-deposit box and whenever the day arrives, she'll try to fulfill your wishes."

Then he turned to me, "Now, Lee, if you'll excuse us, Hal and I have some private business to tend to. Can you give us a few hours alone?"

Could I? How long had it been since I'd spent a couple of hours window-shopping in the mall? It seemed like years. I was delighted to have a little bit of time on my own.

The private business they needed to take care of? Clyde wanted Hal to make a videotape. Actually, three videotapes—one each for Pamela and Sandra, and another one for me. These too would go into the safe-deposit box. Hal was weak but very willing. Clyde proceeded to set up the video camera in the living room, and Hal (wearing his Panama hat to hide his hair loss) told each of us how much he loved us and expressed his hopes and dreams for his girls and his grandchildren.

Clyde didn't know at the time that Hal had only ten days left on this earth. But, oh, how precious those videotapes are! Just thinking about my tape makes my eyes fill with tears—remembering how Hal expressed his love for me. My hands begin to shake, even now, as I picture him commissioning me to continue writing and speaking, and praying for my greater usefulness in the kingdom of God.

I will never be able to thank Clyde enough for urging Hal to leave this precious gift for me. It meant so much to me that I've decided that I too will leave a videotape for the people I love. I urge you to do the same thing. And do it soon. You know, when a person is sick and confronted by death, it's not easy to talk about things like funeral plans. That's why it's so important to do it now, while you are well. Then hide the tape away somewhere for your loved ones to find and view at the proper time.

THE FINAL GOOD-BYE

As it turned out, Hal's funeral was just the way he wanted it. It took place at the Crystal Cathedral, where Dr. Robert Schuller graciously provided everything we needed—and then some. Hal's brother Don was in charge of the service, and Loren Cunningham was there to talk about the good times he and Hal had shared when they were both very young men. Clyde Martin also talked about how important Hal's friendship had been to him.

Because Hal had served as Ronald Reagan's Commissioner of Immigration, the Border Patrol color guard was on hand, standing beside Hal's casket, which was draped with an American flag. Margaret Harvey, who is an immigrant from New Zealand, asked everyone in attendance who was not a natural-born United States citizen to stand—and stand they did—dozens of them all over the great cathedral.

I also managed to say a few words, in what was by far my most difficult speaking engagement ever. Among the things I said:

> "I have piles of precious memories of this Hal Ezell; I always told him he was 'my favorite man.'"

"Marrying him enabled me to raise two fine daughters, Pam and Sandi. And Hal was the one who encouraged me to seek the reunion with my birth-daughter Julie (after twenty-one years), and our family unit was extended."

I also said that during Hal's term as Commissioner of Immigration, he and I had gained a deep appreciation for ethnic peoples and for the freedom America extends to them.

"Was Hal's death untimely?" I asked. "Unfair? Why? we could ask. All I know for sure is that the keys to life and death are in God's hands and He takes no one casually."

I also tried to interject a little bit of humor into this sad, solemn occasion.

"Perhaps you're aware Hal had two other good wives," I said, "fine Christian women who also died due to cancer. Now they are united with Hal in heaven," I said, sighing, "and only God can sort that one out!"

So This Is Normal

Looking back on it now, it seems to me that in the days immediately surrounding Hal's death, I was too numb to fully realize that he was really gone. I'm sure this numb feel-

The presence of the absence of our loved one is everywhere!

ing is a gift God gives to those who are passing through an extraordinarily difficult time. But once the funeral was over, and all the friends and family had gone back home, the truth of Hal's absence hit me like a brick, right between the eyes.

81

I was discovering, as many other bereaved have discovered, that the presence of the absence of our loved one is everywhere!

As I was cleaning up one day, I sighed and said out loud, "Well, Jesus, I guess it's just back to You and me."

His reply came swiftly and strongly, the words ringing in my heart, "It always was."

I was so struck by the truth of that statement that I had to sit down. I realized at that moment that no matter how many friends or family members a person may have, the bottom line always comes down to just two—Jesus and you. Like the old spiritual says, "On the Jericho road, there's room for just two . . . no more and no less, just Jesus and you."[1]

I smiled, through my tears, at the knowledge that Jesus will never turn away from me or leave me, and that, as long as He is with me, I will never be truly alone.

"He who lacks time to mourn lacks time to mend."

And yet, in moments when I'd retreat to our bedroom— I mean *my* bedroom—for some privacy, the loneliness I felt was overwhelming. Hal's jewelry is on the dresser . . . a pair of his shoes await at shoe repair . . . his clothes hang in the closet; what am I supposed to do with them? I would sob into his pillow and cry out for him. He was my life's partner, best friend, chief supporter in the ministry, an excellent husband, father, and grandpa. How could I go on without him? I knew the pain would stay with me for a long, long time, but I also knew that, as Shakespeare said, "He who lacks time to mourn lacks time to mend."[2]

MOURNING LESSONS

In my search for answers to my grief, I discovered that the Jewish people seem to have a better handle on mourning than we goyim. For the orthodox Jew, the grieving process is strictly outlined. In Rabbi Wayne Dosick's work *The Complete Guide to Jewish Belief, Tradition and Practice*, their tradition is clear. The body should be buried (ideally) within twenty-four hours of death, and the primary mourner is to tear his/her garment to reflect a "torn heart." During the first seven days of mourning, the loved one should not leave the house but may receive sympathetic guests. It is customary for the mourner to sit on the floor, or on a low bench, symbolizing "being brought low" in grief, a reminder of ancient days when mourners would sit in sackcloth and ashes.

For eleven months after the funeral, the mourner is to keep all mirrors in his or her home covered and recite the "kaddish" prayer. Only when the first anniversary of the death approaches is the bereaved loved one encouraged to "let go" and return to a more normal existence.

But "returning to a normal existence" is much easier said than done. There's no way things can ever be normal when you have a hole in your life—and a hole in your heart.

Dear reader, is there a hole in your life? If so, make this day count. Do you need to cry? Then cry. Pour out your aching heart to God. Tell Him you want to believe in His goodness again. This "dumping" process is necessary before you can rightly ponder what follows.

Close this book right now, take a break, and take care of some serious business with God.

Asking . . . and Acting!

Step 1: Asking

When you can't figure God out . . . are you disillusioned with Him or awed by Him? If our human minds could totally understand God, wouldn't that bring Him down to our level?

Step 2: Acting

Have you ever prepared an agenda for your own funeral? Maybe it seems a bit morbid right now, but it's a little like saving up for retirement. You won't need it for a long time, but it's good to have it ready! Here are some suggestions to get you started:

1. Write down your desire about the essential elements of your service: your choice of speaker, songs, location.
2. If there is anything you are strongly opposed to, now's the time to say so! For example, you may not want pictures of yourself on display. Perhaps you want your service to be purely worship and not so much of a eulogy. Maybe you don't even want a service! Your wishes should be considered, and by making them known you will help simplify things for your loved ones and minimize the risk of family quarrels.
3. After you have written your agenda, file it in a safe place and tell your closest loved ones where it is.
4. From time to time—maybe at spring cleaning time— get your agenda out and read through it. You may want to make changes as time goes by!

SEVEN

SEEK AND YE SHALL FIND

Wisdom is supreme; therefore get wisdom.
Though it cost all you have, get understanding.

Proverbs 4:7

Numbers.

They've been very much on my mind.

Not too long ago, there was a story in the paper about a woman who was celebrating her one-hundredth birthday. It was a happy occasion, full of family and friends.

One hundred years! That's a long time.

And I got to wondering, why do some people live such a long time, while others—like Hal—die before their time?

Was the psalmist being literal when he wrote, "All the days ordained for me were written in your book before one of them came to be" (Ps. 139:16)?

There are so many verses in the Bible that seem to imply the same thing—that God knows the number of days we will live before we are even born. If this is true, I wondered, why do the good often die so young—those who have so much to offer. Peter Marshall died at forty-seven. Oswald Chambers was forty-three.

Surely these men had much more to offer. Some say, "You don't go until your work is finished," but when I think of the men mentioned above, I just don't see how that can possibly be true. Nevertheless, in a speech at the National Religious Broadcasters' convention, Dr. Billy Graham said he believed that there was a protective covering surrounding him. When the day came when he was supposed to die, that covering would come down, and that would be it. Apparently, the servant of the Lord is quite indestructible until God is through with him.

But then, if God has ordained our days, then does it matter how I live? Does God say, "Okay, I'll give Mary 22,348 days, and Roger gets 19,787?" If so, who cares if I smoke, or eat too much, or don't exercise, because it's not going to help me live longer, right? Or perhaps it is true that God knows what our life-span potential is, but we can extend it or shorten it by our own behavior.

Apparently, the servant of the Lord is quite indestructible until God is through with him.

We've all heard the glib expression when someone dies, "His number was up." But is this biblical? When I asked my Christian friends whether they thought this was really so, most of them said yes. Most of them pointed to Psalm 90 to support their position. But when I looked it up, these verses seemed to be more of a warning to live properly than a proof text that we are all allotted a certain number of days to live—no more and no less.

86

Here's what it says in verse 12: "Teach us to number our days aright, that we may gain a heart of wisdom."

Was my husband destined to go to heaven on the day he died? Is there some arbitrary date written down in the heavenlies, in the Book of Life, which says on what day you will experience the beginning of your eternal life? If so, I should swallow hard and just admit that the botched procedure that was the immediate cause of Hal's death was what God used to take my husband home, period, case closed? There wasn't anything I could have done to change things, so why should I give it another thought? On the other hand, what if that wasn't "his time" to go, but Satan sneaked in there and snatched him away from me? Or what if Hal's death was merely the result of an inept hospital staff?

This kind of thinking led to other questions:

- Did God always know the precise day Charlton Heston (I mean Moses) would deliver the children of Israel from their four hundred years of bondage and slavery?
- Had God preordained the exact day Mary would give birth to Jesus?
- What about Judas Iscariot? If it was preordained that he would betray Christ, then why should we blame him for anything?
- And was the day for the crucifixion preset and predestined?

The conclusion I finally came to was that God knows the time we will die. There are many verses which seem to indicate that this is so:

- "There is . . . a time to be born and a time to die" (Eccles. 3:1–2).
- "Man's days are determined; you have decreed the number of his months and have set limits he cannot exceed" (Job 14:5).

87

- "The LORD brings death and makes alive; he brings down to the grave and raises up" (1 Sam. 2:6).
- "All the days ordained for me were written in your book before one of them came to be" (Ps. 139:16).
- "From one man he made every nation of men, that they should inhabit the whole earth; and he determined the times set for them and the exact places where they should live" (Acts 17:26).

I could only find one case where a man extended his days. God answered King Hezekiah's prayers and added fifteen years to his life. But during those extra years, he got into some big trouble. The story is all there in the twentieth chapter of 2 Kings.

IS GOD IN CONTROL OR NOT?

My search for answers was leading me into some very deep theological waters. But my thirst for truth was insatiable! I finally decided that believing God is in control does not mean that He is sitting up there in heaven plotting against us. He's not dealing out disease, plane crashes, and hurricanes to teach us a lesson. A God who instigates drunk-driver deaths, causes babies to fall in swimming pools and drown, and inflicts people with cancer is not the sort of God anyone could warm up to or worship. No, God does not sin nor tempt anyone else to sin.

Many of these unexplainable events can be analyzed and the source traced. There is a hurricane season in some regions, and the storms will inevitably occur each year. In many cases disease can be traced either to genetics, environmental causes, or mistreatment of our bodies—like smoking, improper diet, or not getting enough exercise. When the people in a country are starving, you can often find man-made reasons for that too.

Yet we must acknowledge that, despite all of these earthly mishaps, God still has control. I believe that He is limiting His involvement because He will not override any-one's free will. We are not just pawns in some celestial chess game. At the same time, I believe He cleans up all the messes we've made and works at turning evil into good for those who love Him.

We have a God who weeps with us when we go through times of pain and sorrow, yet He also explains in His Word that suffering will be a part of living on this planet.

- "We must go through many hardships to enter the kingdom of God" (Acts 14:22).
- "I will show him [Paul] how much he must suffer for my name" (Acts 9:16).
- "You will be counted worthy of the kingdom of God, for which you are suffering" (2 Thess. 1:5).
- "In this world you will have trouble" (John 16:33).

What about airplane disasters? Didn't Jesus promise us, "I am with you always" (Matt. 28:20)? Somehow, after my search through the Scriptures, I'm more relaxed about living now—even on small planes flying through vicious storms. I remember how God says: "'For I know the plans I have for you,' declares the LORD, 'plans to prosper you and not to harm you, plans to give you hope and a future'" (Jer. 29:11).

During the time when I was wrestling with all these diffi-cult questions, I was due to go out of town for a week of speak-ing around the country. I was dreading it because the birth of my sixth grandson, Cooper, was overdue, and I wanted to be home for the birth.

I was fervently praying that he would be born before I had to go, but then I wondered if that prayer was "legal," since Cooper's days were already "numbered," including the day he would be born. And if that date was "etched in stone" so to speak, then why should I be praying that God would change it?

Wow! I was getting a headache from all that thinking!

As it turned out, God showed me a thing or two about numbers—and about His own sense of humor. Cooper was born on 9/9/99, at 9 P.M., and weighed in at a healthy 9 pounds!

I laughed, and I cried when I saw all those nines strung together. Thank You, Lord, for showing me that no matter what happens, You're still in charge of the universe, down to the smallest detail!

WHAT IS HEAVEN REALLY LIKE?

Over the next few weeks and months I found myself becoming obsessed with the idea of heaven. I wanted to know more about it. What was it like? What was Hal doing there all day long? Was he thinking about me and missing me?

Death ends a life, not a relationship.

What if heaven is really the way it's depicted in cartoons, and everyone is floating around on fluffy clouds, strumming on harps? If that were true, Hal would not be heaven's happy camper! Jesus said, "In my Father's house are many mansions" (John 14:2 KJV), so I wondered if Hal was rattling around up there in a big, empty mansion. I had saved the card that came with the floral display sent by singer Pat Boone to Hal's funeral. Pat had written on the card, "Enjoy your mansion, Hal; I hope we'll be neighbors in heaven."

My curiosity about heaven was spurred in part by my grandson Mason, who had more questions about it than Heinz has varieties.

"Is Papa still sick?"

90

"No, Mason, he's completely well."

"Is he naked?"

"No, honey, he's wearing a robe."

"Is he singing in a choir?"

"Maybe he is."

"Are they playing games in heaven?"

"I don't know, Mason. Maybe so."

"Well, if they are, I'll bet God is playing with Jesus, and Papa is playing with Abraham Lincoln!"

Thank you, Mason, for the laughter.

During this time, I caught the very end of a TV interview with Billy Graham. When the interviewer asked Dr. Graham what he thought heaven would be like, the great evangelist replied, "In heaven, I just know no one will be able to point their finger at God and accuse Him of being unfair, because by the time we arrive, all things will be made perfectly clear to us."

I also found some solid answers about heaven in Dr. Erwin W. Lutzer's book, *One Minute After You Die*:

> There is no evidence that those in heaven can actually see us on earth, though that might be possible. It is more likely that they can ask for regular updates on how we are doing down here. I cannot imagine that such a request would be denied, but once in heaven we will soon get to meet a host of others. . . .
>
> On the Mount of Transfiguration, three of the disciples met Moses and Elijah. And as far as we know, there was no need for name tags.[1]

I also liked what Randy Alcorn had to say about heaven in his imaginative novel, *Dominion*:

> Heaven does not make your mind duller, but sharper. You are aware of the rebellion on earth and the ugliness of hell. Happiness here does not depend on ignorance of reality. It depends on having God's perspective on reality.[2]

It gives me great comfort to think that we will be able to recognize our loved ones in heaven, and be recognized by them. When I get to heaven, I am still going to be me, and you are still going to be you. Although, I believe we will be vastly improved, in every way, over the frail, clumsy creatures we are while we're living on this physical plane.

I just wonder what age we'll be in heaven. (I hope it's the age before about everything starts to sag and deteriorate.)

But even though I believe we will still be "ourselves" in heaven, I also tend to think that we will be recognized more by who we really are—by the spirit inside us—than by what we look like. It seems like what we truly are overpowers what we look like anyway.

The Bible does tell us a few things about heaven. There will be rivers, hills, streets of gold, cities of diamonds, and gates of pearl. We know that we will eat in heaven (hooray!), and that there will be no night, because Jesus is the light.

We also know that:

1. Death offers us no chance to try again (sorry, no reincarnation). But the best news about heaven is that we'll definitely be with Jesus! Because when we are absent from the body, we'll be in the presence of the Lord.
2. Whatever ties we had on earth that have been broken by death will be restored there—and not only restored, but strengthened many times beyond what we ever thought was possible.
3. We can trust the apostle Paul's description of heaven, when he said: "No eye has seen, no ear has heard, no mind has conceived what God has prepared for those who love him" (1 Cor. 2:9). Even Steven Spielberg couldn't depict it!
4. There will be no entrance exam for heaven; no Bible trivia quiz. No "can you name the books of the Bible?" No, "What church were you a member of?" None of that. I'm sure the entry requirement would be short

and simple; it would all be about the cross of Christ. Only one question would be asked: "What did you do with my son, Jesus Christ?"

Another thing we know about heaven is that it will be the place where all our questions about suffering are finally answered. It may not be like this, but I love this story from a Calvary Chapel pastor, Don McClure.

Picture a big tent beyond the pearly gates with the sign *All People with Questions Here*. Of course, we get in line. We've been waiting to find out why we had to suffer. As your turn comes, you step up to the panel assembled to deal with your questions. Panel members include:

Joseph, who was betrayed by his brothers and unjustly imprisoned.

Moses, who spent forty years leading the murmuring Israelites through the wilderness.

Naomi, who lost her husband and her sons.

Job, who lost his fortune and his family.

Isaiah, who was sawn in half.

Peter, who was crucified upside down.

Stephen, who was stoned to death.

But the panel member who speaks up first is John the Baptist. He asks, "Now, what suffering did you go through?"

ALONE AT CHRISTMAS

Prior to Hal's death, Christmas was always one of my favorite holidays. I loved everything about it. The lights, the carols, even the crowds in the mall.

But not this year.

It seemed as if every time I turned on the radio, I heard a song that made me cry.

Blue Christmas . . . I'll Be Home for Christmas . . . Merry Christmas, Darling . . . I never realized before how many sad Christmas songs there are, or how many Christmas songs have to do with romantic love. They brought back so many memories of times spent with my beloved husband—cuddling in front of the fireplace, worshiping God together in a candlelit Christmas Eve service, shopping for toys for the grandkids, opening our presents together on Christmas morning. My loneliness was so intense that I actually felt physical pain. How I missed my Hal!

During this time, a friend sent me a poem that was written by a thirteen-year-old boy named Ben, just before he died of a brain tumor in December of 1997. His poem was a tremendous comfort to me and, I'm sure, to thousands of others who read it. In part, he wrote:

My First Christmas in Heaven
I see the countless Christmas trees
around the world below
with tiny lights, like heaven's stars,
reflecting on the snow.
The sight is so spectacular.
Please wipe away your tear,
for I am spending Christmas
with Jesus Christ this year.

I hear the many Christmas songs
that people hold so dear,
but that music can't compare
with the Christmas choir up here.
I have no words to tell you,
the joy their voices bring—
for it is beyond description,
to hear the angels sing.

I know how much you miss me,
I see the pain in your heart,
but I am not so far away;
we're really not that far apart.
So be happy for me, my family;

you know I hold you dear.
And be glad that I'm spending Christmas
with Jesus this year.

Please love and keep each other,
as our Father said to do.
For I can't count the blessings or love
He has for each of you.
So have a Merry Christmas,
and wipe away that tear,
'cause remember I'm spending Christmas
with Jesus Christ this year!

I believe that if we truly knew what waited for us on "the other side," we would not cling so tenaciously to life here on earth, nor would we grieve so deeply for those who are now enjoying life on "the other side." I'll bet Hal's entry to heaven was fascinating.

In my mind's eye, I can see the line forming to greet him:

"Thanks, Hal! I would have been aborted before I was ever born if you hadn't helped at that crisis pregnancy center."

"I'm so glad to meet you. You helped straighten out my immigration problems so I could come to America—as a missionary from Romania."

"Thanks for telling me about Jesus. That's the reason I'm here!

🌿 Asking . . . and Acting!

Step 1: Asking

Psalm 116:15 says, "Precious in the sight of the Lord is the death of his saints." What does this verse mean to you?

Step 2: Acting

For the Christian, death will not be an end, but a joyous beginning. Do you have friends and relatives waiting for you in heaven? If so, why not make a list of all the people you look forward to seeing again (or for the first time) when you get there?

For Bible Study

1 Samuel 2:6
2 Kings 20
Job 14:5
Psalms 90; 139:16
Proverbs 4:7
Ecclesiastes 3:1–2

Jeremiah 29:11
John 14:2; 16:33
Acts 9:16; 14:22; 17:26
2 Thessalonians 1:5
1 Corinthians 2:9

EIGHT

GRACE COMES IN THE MOURNING

You don't realize Jesus is all you need . . .
until Jesus is all you have.

Alone.

"Without company; solitary. Excluding all others." That's how Funk and Wagnall's dictionary defines the word *alone*.

At times, it seemed I was living a surreal existence—I could see everything happening around me, but I felt disconnected from it. Even worse . . . disinterested in it. I was numb with shock and grief. It was a state I was totally unprepared to deal with.

I used to think of myself as strong, independent, self-sufficient. Being alone didn't intimidate me at all because I had been there before, more than once.

In fact, when it came to being alone, I could have been America's poster child. Let me tell you just a little bit about those early years, the years of . . .

LIFE BEFORE HAL

I learned to be independent early in life. I was the third of five children—all girls. My sisters and I did not grow up with a positive father figure in our lives. Our father was an alcoholic, and our entire family was affected by his addiction.

As my teenage years progressed, I became more and more determined to break free as soon as possible. My older sister Zoe had already married and moved to California, and after much urging, I finally convinced my mother that we should leave my dad and our unhappy existence behind and head west too. Even though my mother had endured years of beatings, both verbal and physical, it was hard for her to take this step. I was only seventeen years old, but it fell upon me to take the lead as we packed and moved to San Francisco.

Of course, I hoped that life would be better in San Francisco. And at first, things fell nicely into place. I found a job as a secretary for a boat manufacturer and enjoyed the other ladies I worked with. But then one terrible day, I was raped by a man who worked as a subcontractor for my company, and "alone" took on a deeper, more devastating dimension for me.

I won't go into all of the details of the next few years of my life here. Let me just say that I left San Francisco pregnant from that rape and went south to Los Angeles to have my baby and make sure she was adopted by people who could take better care of her than I could at that time in my life. What I *do* want to tell you is that on the way to Los Angeles, I stopped to spend the night in a crummy motel. I still remember the despair I felt as I stretched my tired body out on the bed. I felt the need to talk to someone, but there was no one to confide in.

Except God. I had responded to Him before we left Pennsylvania, when a few of my friends and I attended a Billy Graham Crusade one weekend because we were bored. I received Christ as my Savior that night. But it was in that dreary hotel room, a most unlikely place to fellowship with the Creator of the universe, that I began to lean on Him. Throughout that night, I talked to Him and read His Word. To my amazement, He responded by leading me to the words I needed to help me surrender my hopeless mess to Him. A peace flooded my soul that I had never before known, and when I resumed my drive to Los Angeles, I did so with new-found confidence that *I was no longer alone!*

The amazing story of how God took care of me and later restored me to my beautiful, lost daughter is told in my book *The Missing Piece.* I mention it only briefly here to show that I had weathered my share of life's storms.

But still, after Hal's death, I was totally unprepared for my reaction the first time I walked into our favorite Italian restaurant and heard the waiter say, "Table for one?"

TABLE FOR ONE!

I totally lost it. The full impact of being alone hit me in a new and different way, rushing over me like a flood and washing away that confidence and security that had helped me successfully "ride the waves" so many times in the past. But, you see, during my years of marriage with Hal, his life and my life merged inseparably into *one* life. With his passing a part of me died, and that brought into play a whole new definition of being alone. This time I wasn't just on my own . . . "you and me, God." Half of me was gone, and now I had to learn who *I* was and how to cope with being single again.

Unless God has given you the gift of singleness, going solo in our society is at best a challenge. I remember the years and years of waiting and longing for that special man to come into my life. It wasn't an easy time. But this "suddenly single" state was infinitely harder for me to cope with than my former state of being "still single."

Just as you can't put perfume back into a bottle once its fragrance has been poured out, you can't simply go back to "being single" when you lose your mate. The very essence of Lee Ezell—my unique "fragrance"—had been poured out. This was a far lonelier state than anything I had ever experienced.

Go . . . and Grow

I have several goals in mind for the remainder of this chapter. I want to share with you the more-or-less haphazard process I went through as I grieved, grew, and rediscovered myself. It is my hope that my experiences will encourage you and perhaps give you some practical help in dealing with your own current grief. (I also urge you to see the Widow's Appendix in the back of the book.)

A deep sense of loss can be experienced through more than the loss of a spouse, of course. You may be grieving over a rebellious child, the death of a friend, even the loss of a job you loved.

If you are not grieving right now, perhaps my book will help you be more effective in supporting someone you know who is grieving or prepare you for such a time that will inevitably come in your own life.

And I also hope to challenge you to *never* stop clinging to God—even though you might be filled with confusion, questions, and even anger over life's unfairness. "In your anger do not sin," God tells us (Eph. 4:26). That is His invitation to us. To deny our confusion and anger would only be a form of lying, and "don't lie" is one of the few hard-and-fast commandments He gives us.

It is only as we learn to be honest with God, trusting Him all the while to see us through and answer our toughest questions, that our relationship with Him becomes authentic. As we *go* with Him through our grief, we also *grow*. And, as we lean on Him—not in weak denial, but in active trust—His staying grace will surely come.

Permission Granted

If you are grieving right now, that's okay. No, better than okay. It is normal and natural. To submerge your feelings or cover them up would be a disastrous thing to do, so give yourself permission to grieve. Let the tears flow, allow the process to run its course toward healing. Don't let others shut you down, insinuating that you should be over it by now. Grief buried is buried alive. So let it hit you and knock you down, then walk through it. Only then can you hope to stand on the other side.

Seek out true friends who will allow you to grieve whenever it hits you. When I was speaking in England, a proper English woman approached me and confessed her embarrassment about her tears. "So sorry," she said. "I haven't felt permission to release my grief until I heard you speaking about being a widow. At my church they seem to feel I should be 'over it' by now and are very intolerable if I tear up. So I've just been holding it in, telling myself to move on."

"But this is just the reason you can't move on," I argued. "You are so clogged up with grief that your emotions are plugged up. You must process your grief—whether those chaps like it or not. No, you are not done yet. And you have nothing to be ashamed about. You are right on schedule."

As she cried on my shoulder, I wondered how many others have been scorned and need to be given permission to mourn.

During this time of grief you may feel your life is a bit out of control, because you will wrestle with depression and anger. Your energy level may be low and you may feel yourself reeling from the emotional roller coaster you are on. Your power to make decisions is just temporarily impaired as you mourn. Remind yourself that all these feelings will change. Your emotions will stabilize. You *will* get back to normal! Indeed, you'll be better than normal for having gone through this experience. Believe it or not, this may be your opportunity to grow spiritually.

Let's be honest. We usually cling to God during periods of trial. Few of us are noble enough to seek after God when everything is going our way. We're not a very impressive lot. Now's our chance.

Let me share some of my own journey to the other side of grief.

WHO AM I, ANYWAY?

While Hal was with me, I really had no clue just how much he was, as the song says, "the wind beneath my wings." After his death, I continued to float along, but I sensed no wind—I was powerless and without direction. I had been "Hal's wife" for so long that I couldn't remember who *I* was. We used to have a cherished red plate we'd put on our dinner table for special occasions. On the back of the plate, we wrote notes to commemorate these times. But a visitor who was helping us after Hal's death inadvertently put the plate in the dishwasher and the notes were washed off. I felt as if all of our precious memories went down the drain.

I guess you might say I went through an identity crisis! I always chose my clothes to suit my husband, a man of impeccable taste. Now the simple task of choosing something to wear sent me into an anxiety attack! I couldn't even think of what hobbies I used to enjoy, nor could I decide how to rearrange the house.

I found that tasks that were once simple routines were now "mourning rituals" that triggered painful memories and crippling melancholy. For instance, for many weeks as I made my king-sized bed each day, I would remember sharing that bed with Hal.

There were other rituals too, like fixing meals and doing laundry. It was just me now, and I didn't really *have* to do these things so regularly, but I continued to go through the motions just as if Hal were still there. Somehow there was comfort in keeping things the same.

102

At first, performing these rituals gave me a false sensation that nothing was different. But eventually I experienced what Gerald Sittser describes in his book *A Grace Disguised:* "The initial deluge of loss slowly gave way . . . to the steady seepage of pain that comes when grief, like floodwaters refusing to subside, finds every crack and crevice of the human spirit to enter and erode."[1]

When we are filled to overflowing with grief, it's only natural to want to blame someone else. In my case, the villain I resented was the medical community. The system had let me down, and I wanted more than just the satisfaction of nursing a grudge. Nothing less than "a pound of flesh" would satisfy my need for revenge. So after I recovered from the funeral, I wrote letters of complaint against medical boards, insurance companies, and chiefs of staff. All to no avail. A pile of polite replies accumulated on my counter, reminding me that by law, I could not even be informed if disciplinary action were taken. I'd never even know if I got my pound of flesh or not. How frustrating!

But eventually, despite my feelings of anger and resentment, I made a deliberate decision to forgive. I chose not to allow a root of bitterness to grow and choke away my spiritual life. I could only surmise that all the medical blunders committed during Hal's last days on earth may have been part of God's plan to save him from prolonged suffering and a more agonizing death.

ONE STEP FORWARD, TWO STEPS BACK

I soon learned that grieving is a tedious process. I'd make steps forward, like the choice to forgive, but then something would happen that would hurl me back to square one. Like the time my little grandson Mason was visiting and noticed Hal's electric shaver still on the sink. Pointing to it, Mason asked, "Is that Papa's shaver?"

Gulping down a colossal lump in my throat I answered nonchalantly, "Why yes, Mason. It is Papa's shaver."

Children are so uninhibited, and Mason had no problem with letting his curiosity all hang out. "Do you think it still has Papa's hair in it? Can I see?"

Okay, Lee, you can handle this, I thought, applying a little mental "self-talk" to keep myself from melting into a pile of tears before my inquisitive kindergartner.

"Let's take a look," I said to Mason as I opened the shaver. Sure enough, a pile of fuzz that was once Hal's beard dumped out on the sink. How odd to see this remnant of my husband's daily routine still lingering in my bathroom. And what I wouldn't give to feel his scratchy stubble against my cheek just one more time!

Experiences like these set me back, opening the wound that was slowly healing. Another time I found myself glaring at an elderly couple strolling through the mall, holding hands and laughing like teenagers. The green-eyed monster of jealousy raised up its ugly head. I couldn't bear to think my dream of growing old with Hal would never be realized. Just when we'd finally raised our kids and were looking forward to ice-cream stops together while strolling in the mall, our plans were sabotaged by death. I felt cheated. Why did God allow this couple to have what I wanted so deeply?

I later heard about a grieving widow who was at the grocery store. Her husband of thirty-seven years, Rudy—who had died eight days earlier—had often come to the store with her. And when he did, he would wander off while she did her weekly shopping. When he came back, he'd have three yellow flowers for her because he knew how much she loved them.

On this particular occasion, a young wife was standing in front of the meat counter, trying to make up her mind. "My husband loves T-bones," she said, "but at these prices, I just don't know."

The widow swallowed hard and said, "My husband just passed away. Buy the steaks and cherish every moment you have with him." The woman smiled sympathetically and told the butcher she'd take two of his best steaks.

Later, when the widow reached the checkout counter, she was surprised to discover that the other woman was waiting for her with three yellow roses.

"These are to thank you for your advice," she said.

"Oh, Rudy," the widow smiled through her tears. "You haven't forgotten me, have you?"

Stories like this one comforted me in my loss.

But then I'd be sent reeling back to square one by one of those special events that creeps up on the calendar and just seems to hit you like a slap in the face. As each "first" passed by—Mother's Day, Father's Day, our birthdays and anniversary—I tried my best to scamper through. It was a feeble effort at best.

I would grow forward . . . and go backward, without even a predictable pattern. I was stuck in a rut, and it seemed at times that I'd never really get past "Go."

OUT ON THE ROAD AGAIN

But, go I must! Just two months after Hal died I was scheduled to speak four times in Indianapolis at the Gaither Praise Gathering—Hal's favorite meeting. When Gloria Gaither called and graciously offered to release me from this commitment, I was tempted to accept. But I couldn't postpone for long my return to speaking, and I had already received disgruntled reactions from some groups during the early weeks of grieving when I simply could not fulfill my obligations. So out on the road I went, once again, feeling weaker and more inadequate than ever before. At times I wondered if I could actually keep going. I was billed as a "humor therapist," and the last thing I felt like doing was making folks laugh. Did God really want me to continue, in spite of my grief?

The Gaither Gathering proved to be a blessing with burdened moments. It was wonderful to link up with so many old friends—to enjoy the warmth of fellowship and laughter like I couldn't find anywhere else. But then there were those awkward moments when people would come looking for Hal, not knowing he had just moved to heaven.

I remember gulping hard when a precious old gospel singer named Jake Hess asked, "Where's my friend, Hal?"

"Jake, he is with Jesus," I replied.

A brief look of surprise flashed across his face, but he didn't hesitate before saying, "You mean Hal beat me to the Banquet Table?" Then tears of compassion flowed as he hugged me.

Others sought me out, intent on comforting me. One well-meaning elderly woman said, "Oh, Lee, I can relate! I lost my precious dog last summer, and I miss him so badly."

Now I have to admit that my first reaction to this well-meaning lady was to want to punch her lights out! How could she even speak of the loss of her pet in the same sentence as my indescribable loss? Then I realized her dog may have been her only loving companion, and her grief over that loss was probably very deep.

Still another gentleman asked me, "How long did your husband suffer?"

"Fourteen weeks," I replied, trying hard not to remember those suffering days.

I felt numb when he cheerfully remarked, "What a blessing that he went so fast!" I couldn't believe anyone would have the nerve to actually say that to me. But then he shared how his wife had battled through years of agonizing suffering before she died. As God gave me a different perspective through this man's experienced eyes, I was able to see that fourteen weeks of suffering *was* a blessing. How hard it would have been to endure weeks, months, and years of wondering when the pain would end.

Another time I found myself weeping as I talked with one of Hal's old friends. He flatly commented, "You're religious, aren't you?" Almost impatiently, it seemed.

"Of course," I replied quickly.

"Well . . . then?" he said inquisitively. As if to say, "So why the tears?"

Although I knew this man was trying to help me pull myself up by the bootstraps, I wanted to retort defensively that when we weep for those we've lost it's not about the one who's gone. I wasn't weeping for Hal. My tears were for me—my own personal loss of a companion, a friend, a mate. Religious or not, he couldn't expect me to not be human. To deny that we feel loss is to be dishonest with ourselves, others, and God.

This wonderful Gaither Gathering turned out to be a turning point for me and a time when God began to answer some of my questions. One memorable moment came when Ken Medema, a man blind from birth, ministered a word of wisdom to me. As I greeted him at his keyboard, I told him what a struggle it was for me to continue speaking while I was consumed with grief over the loss of my husband. Ken slipped a tape into his keyboard and simply said, "Maybe this will help."

On the spot, impromptu, this musician composed a beautiful song . . . *for me!* I am convinced beyond a doubt that Ken Medema was God's microphone and that He was bending down to sing a song of comfort in my ear. Later I titled it *I'll Be There*, and here is an excerpt:

I'm puttin' on my speakin' suit again.
Try not to be too conscious of the pain.
The man I loved was taken; it seems to be so cruel,
And now I'm showing up for work and I'm feeling like a
    fool.
Do I think that I can make it through this day?
Through all the inane things people will say?
They'll have not a ghost of an idea—
They won't know what I'm going through.
So they'll prattle on about this 'n that

And I'll wish I could run right out of the room.
But I know I'll do what God wants me to do.
I'll be here—'cause I promised You.
I'll be here—doing what I'm called to do.

A spark of courage ignited in my heart through this song.
From the day Ken sang that song, I have not looked back.
I started to *suit* up and *show* up at my speaking engagements.
At times I felt weak and on the edge, not half as confident
as I appeared. But weakness is the prerequisite to being able
to learn the secret of God's power being made perfect in
my weakness. And always I prayed—and still do—for an
anointing to do whatever God wanted me to do for the
audience He sent me to address. And I'm using all my unfair
experiences to illustrate God's faithfulness.

I have tasted grief but not wasted grief.

ONE DAY AT A TIME

Fulfilling my full-time speaking schedule was a baby step
of faith toward healing. But I still had an uphill climb ahead
of me, and believe me, it was a Matterhorn! Theoretically,
I was well-prepared to resume single life. After all, I had
been on my own for many years before I married Hal and
had proven early in life that I was capable of taking care of
myself. Still, I found that making decisions—big or small—
sent me into a panic of insecurity.

Now I'm about to tell you something with fear and trem-
bling. There are some Christians who may not take kindly
to this confession . . . some who may even accuse me of
being disrespectful to Jesus. So at great risk of being stoned
by modern-day Pharisees, here goes.

You know those bracelets with the initials W.W.J.D. that kids wear to remind them to stop and think, "What would Jesus do?" Well, for a while I found it helpful to wear a bracelet similar in style and purpose. Only mine had the letters W.W.H.D? Can you guess what the "H" stood for? Right on . . . Hal. What would Hal do? Somehow, in those perplexing moments when I just didn't have a clue, it helped me tremendously to look at my bracelet and stop and think about what my clever, practical husband would do if he were here. I missed talking things over with Hal so much. He was my chief adviser, my counselor, and like the guiding needle on a compass, my "true north." When I took the time to stop and think through what Hal would do, it was easier to make my own decision. I believe that as I thought through what Hal would do, Jesus was continuing to use the memories of my departed husband to help me cope. I share this little tip with you because it was a practice that helped me to let go of Hal, bit by bit. A strange thing happened in the process too, because releasing my earthly husband caused me to lean more on my *heavenly* husband, Jesus Christ.

Through all of this, I was discovering that grief is a process. A process of moving forward and sliding back. The good news is that, as we persevere, the ultimate outcome is healing. As the weeks bled into months, I hit one significant "down day" that proved to be a breakthrough. As I turned to God's Word in search of comfort, I discovered a verse that was new to me. "For your Maker is your husband," says the prophet Isaiah (54:5). And then I found this passage in the Book of Hosea, "I will betroth you to me forever; I will betroth you in righteousness and justice, in love and compassion" (Hosea 2:19).

Wow! What a revolutionary thought! Just as God had met me in a dingy hotel room years before and given me what I needed to go on, so He met me again. Suddenly I felt like chains were falling off of me. Hope surged through me like an electric current as I realized that God is not only my friend, my brother, and my master but also my husband. A husband so perfect and faithful that not even my wonderful Hal could compare.

Through His Word, I was encouraged to find that this heavenly husband would always listen (Ps. 116:1–2), would never leave me (Heb. 13:5), would forgive me everything (1 John 1:9), and would never ever push me beyond my limitations (1 Cor. 10:13). No guy has a track record like that!

So I began to develop this spousal relationship with God. I found myself asking Him for all kinds of advice and input about finances and for help to get things done—anything and everything. Like any wife would, I complained to Him, fussed about things, and often pouted. I was using my God-husband more like a sounding board or as a heavenly "Mr. Fix-It" for my needs. I expected Him to make things right, meet my needs, and fill in the gaps.

But this is not all that a marriage relationship is about! I remember the morning I awoke and began talking out loud to the Lord—making that day's "to do" list for Him. As I quoted Him the Scripture I was relying on, God clearly caught me up short by speaking these words to me: *If you want me to be your husband, then act like a bride.*

Ouch! I hadn't considered what a fishwife I must have sounded like to God. Although He was to fill in for my husband, He was not to be my fairy godmother, nor my sugar daddy. He is the Bridegroom.

This experience changed me. My conversations with Him became more considerate, more loving. I would awaken to tell God how glad I was to have Him with me each day and that I knew nothing could separate me from His love. I became more grateful, a spouse who counted her blessings more than her wants. As a result, instead of the grueling daily "to do" list, I'd find myself just reviewing my day ahead with Him and asking for His input. I'd tell Him I would change anything to please Him, if He would just indicate to me what He wanted. Our relationship became closer, and I felt more cared for and less worried.

RENEWING MY VOWS

I decided to renew my marriage vows and pledge my troth—whatever that is—to this perfect Husband, and so in a quiet, personal ceremony, I repeated the familiar pledge.

> I take you, Lord,
> To have and to hold
> From this day forward
> For better or for worse
> For richer or for poorer
> In sickness and in health
> To love and to cherish . . .
> FOREVER!

Not even death could separate me from this husband! And suddenly I realized that even though I was physically alone, I had never been less alone in my life than in that moment when I affirmed my union with God, my Husband.

My official "marriage" to God made the grieving easier, but still I had to face that painful landmark—the one-year anniversary of Hal's death. As it neared, I made a decision I hoped God would approve of. I needed to see an end to the intensity of my grieving. To the crying in the night. To the delicate emotional state I was in. So I asked God to help me process the bulk of my grief by the one-year anniversary date. Then I deliberately went through a "ritual of closure." I went back to his grave and dumped some more of it there. I took the guest registry books from the mortuary and funeral and read the names of all the friends and family who came to honor Hal. I took old pictures and laughed and cried over them.

When I returned home, I watched the precious videotape Hal had made for me. This was an extremely emotional experience, but a precious one. I determined to mark that day as a new beginning, and so I switched my wedding ring to my right hand. It was a harder job than I anticipated (and I don't just mean squeezing the ring over my knuckle). In a deliberate and symbolic act, I placed "Mrs. Hal Ezell" on

Grace outlives the mourning.

the altar, hoping she would be consumed by the fire of the Spirit. I prayed that Lee would rise up with new fire in her belly. I needed a date to mark the beginning of my life as a single and the end of my grieving as a widow. God was so good! On the one-year anniversary, He gave me a precious verse I hang on to. It's one for you too:

> I will give you the treasures of darkness,
>   riches stored in secret places,
> so that you may know that I am the LORD,
>   the God of Israel, who summons you by name.
>
> Isaiah 45:3

BEYOND THE MOURNING

I was finally moving on, and it felt good. Interestingly enough, I discovered that there's another definition of *alone* in Funk and Wagnall's dictionary. It goes like this: "Without equal; unique; unparalleled: 'as an artist, he stands alone.'"

With God as my husband, I was learning that being alone can be a state "without equal." I'm not saying it's easy, but it's something to strive for. And I *am* saying He'll help me as I strive. Believe me, I have learned that grace outlives the mourning.

Asking . . . and Acting!

Step 1: Asking

When I "let go" and move on, am I abandoning my loved one or learning to love him in a new way? As I put closure on grief, don't I also open myself to sweet memories I couldn't bear while grieving?

Step 2: Acting

As you go through the grief process, you may want to schedule a time (a day, a weekend, etc.) when you perform a personal ritual of letting go. Here's a prayer you can personalize by inserting the name of your lost loved one. You may have to perform this ritual more than once, but each time you will be taking the situation a little more in stride and moving toward the day when you finally let go.

Dear heavenly Father,
Today I offer You my pain and grief over the loss of _____. I am attempting to let go and reach out for Your healing. I ask You to take away the agony of this loss and replace it with a sense of Your loving presence. And even though _____ is no longer in my life, I know I am not alone. I walk away from this time believing You are holding my hand. Thank You for receiving me and relieving me because of the sacrifice of my Lord, Jesus Christ. Amen.

Later, why not have coffee with a supportive, understanding friend? Take time to share the experiences of your time alone. Getting into the Light with someone can be so healing.

Then have a deliberate celebration! You have processed a bunch of grief baggage, and now your load will be lighter.

May you find comfort in your memories!

FOR BIBLE STUDY

Psalm 116:1–2
Isaiah 54:5
Hosea 2:19
1 Corinthians 10:13
Ephesians 4:26
Hebrews 13:5
1 John 1:9

NINE

AFTERSHOCK

Earth has no sorrow that heaven cannot heal.

Thomas Moore

Shaken.

If you've ever had the good fortune to live through a major earthquake, you know that a great deal of the rockin' and rollin' comes later. For days, weeks, months . . . yes, even years . . . there are aftershocks. The initial quake may cause great structural damage, and people go to work immediately to repair and rebuild. But if an earthquake ever hits where you live, be forewarned! Just when you finally calm down and begin to rebuild, there may be an aftershock— and some are stronger than the initial earthquake. All the progress you've made may come tumbling down around you in a heap of rubble. In California, where I live, we expect it. It's part of the package deal here!

This analogy was far removed from my mind when the shaking started in my life . . . *again.* It was just a regular checkup. No symptoms. No fears or worries about my health.

Just that routine, albeit unpleasant, "girl thing" you have to do every year.

Only this time, the routine checkup turned up unexpected results. I was in a hurry that day. It wasn't in my plans to be delayed by a diligent, determined radiological technologist, but after doing the routine mammogram she informed me they needed to retake the images. She thought she saw something, and she just wanted to make sure. Oh, brother!

I knew my family health history made me a high-risk patient. My mother and one of my sisters are both breast cancer victims, but I honestly believed that the blood of Christ would shield me from that genetic connection. So even when the technician insisted on doing a *third* mammogram that day, I wasn't buying it.

I'm afraid I got a bit testy with the technician *and* the radiologist. Later I would return to present them both with chocolates to thank them for being persistent and saving my life. Right now, though, I was late to an appointment and just wanted to put my clothes on and go.

Finally, after a sonogram, the health professionals affirmed the existence of a suspicious mass of fibrous breast tissue. A biopsy was scheduled, performed, the results came in and . . . *wham!* The emotional Richter scale went wild. On my birthday, ten weeks after Hal's funeral, I was told that I too had cancer.

Some birthday present, eh? I drove home in a stupor, my head spinning with questions. Could such an irony be possible? Would a loving God allow such a thing to happen to me? A million questions surged through my brain as I fought hard to process the opening ceremony for this new major life crisis.

I recalled at once that prior to me, Hal had been married to two women who died of cancer. I vowed long ago that I would not perpetuate this tradition. My friends were still weary from bearing my burdens of suffering and grief through Hal's ordeal. How could I tell them the nightmare was starting all over again?

IS THERE A DOCTOR IN THE HOUSE?

One of the hardest things to face about this soul-shaking news was the necessity to become involved with the medical community again. I could barely face this. I had serious issues with the oncologist who treated Hal, so I breathed a sigh of relief when I discovered that my HMO insurance plan allowed me a choice.

The other oncologist on my plan was a physician named Dr. Erin Lang. Hmm . . . so far, so good. At least the name implied that this doctor might speak coherent English. In my mind I pictured a vibrant, red-headed, hot-blooded Irishman. Yes, indeed! I could communicate with a doctor named Erin Lang, and so I made an appointment.

I had vowed I would never set foot through the doors to that cancer center again, but here I was experiencing déjà vu. It was no dream; I had been here before. As I filled out new patient forms, I came to the place that said . . .

Check one: ___Married   ___Single ___Widowed

OUCH! Would the hurt never go away? Married felt so safe, secure, and connected. Single? That meant available, with all the exciting possibilities. But widowed? To me that was merely a code word for pain, loneliness, and loss.

It seemed chilly in the exam room as I waited for my Irish doctor to make an entrance. Imagine my surprise when he entered and in a thick Chinese accent said, "Hello, I Dr. Lang. I very glad for meet you."

For a moment I stared in disbelief. Apparently it was a reaction Dr. Lang was used to because he smiled and said, "Many people think because of my name I am Caucasian, but I'm born Taiwan."

My heart sank a notch, but I could see he had a caring manner, and in my many travels to Taiwan I had grown to deeply love and respect these valiant Chinese people who had escaped from Communist China. So I practiced my best Taiwanese on him and promised to bring him a Chinese translation of one of my books. Things were warming up now!

I felt I owed Dr. Lang an honest and straightforward explanation of what I had been through during the past year and how it had left me feeling disillusioned with the medical profession. I spoke slowly and deliberately—even a little apologetically. I asked if he would be willing to be my "partner in wellness" and emphasized that I wanted to play an active role in the decision-making process concerning my case. I told him that even though I respected his professional experience, I would exercise the right to research every aspect of his recommendations and investigate other options for alternative or complimentary treatments. I told him I was a Christian and did not fear death. I implored him to be truthful with me and to fully disclose details about my condition as we became allies in a fight against the dreaded "C" disease. After making sure I had not forgotten anything, I looked at him and asked if he would shake my hand in a pledge to tell me the whole truth and nothing but the truth.

I'm sure Dr. Lang was inwardly thinking something like, "How did I get stuck with *this* patient?" But, to his credit, he extended his hand and said, "Okay, you got it! I gonna tell you the truth—bottom line, I promise."

Relief burst over me like the sun breaking through a cloud. So I agreed to meet with a surgeon of Dr. Lang's choosing to arrange removal of the cancerous mass. He also explained that he would like to have a plastic surgeon standing by in the operating room in the event that reconstructive surgery was necessary.

For the moment, the shaking subsided. But even then I knew there would be many other aftershocks in the days and weeks to come.

PROFESSIONAL OPINIONS

Nothing gets my blood running quite so much as a head-on collision with a doctor! As promised, I kept my appointment with the plastic surgeon Dr. Lang referred me to. While waiting to meet with him, I found myself studying "before and after" photos of face-lifts, tummy tucks and boob jobs and becoming more and more uneasy. After the examination, I asked the surgeon what percentage of his surgeries were cancer-related.

"Well, Mrs. Ezell, this *is* Southern California," he answered glibly. "Most of my surgeries are elective. Maybe 10 percent are cancer patients. So what size breasts would you like?"

"Hold on," I retorted. "I'm not interested in looking like Dolly Parton! I want the smallest possible procedure—a lumpectomy."

It was his "professional" opinion, however, that I should have both breasts removed—to be certain that the cancer would not return or spread to the other breast.

"It's the *only* way to eliminate the risk," he said matter-of-factly. "How about Wednesday at 3 P.M.?"

"The *only* way?" I repeated.

"Yes," came the reply.

At that point, I decided to exercise my right to a *second* professional opinion! So I thanked him, promised to get back to him, then made a beeline to Dr. Lang's office. Who cared if I didn't have an appointment? I'd wait as long as necessary to get a few moments of his time. Finally I was able to look him in the eye and remind him of our solemn pact. "Tell me the truth, please. Is it really true that the *only* way to be risk-free is to have both of my breasts removed?"

Swallowing hard, he replied hesitatingly, "No, Mrs. Ezell. In your case, if cancer returns to area, it will come to lungs or chest wall. It doesn't matter you have breasts or not. Many women fear so much cancer, they choose radical surgery.

119

Is a common choice to have peace. Is necessary in some cases, but not all."

The silence was deafening as I thought about my options. "My decision, then, is to *not* have a plastic surgeon in the operating room. I want the least invasive procedure possible. Understood?"

"Okay," he sighed. "I write in your chart, and we schedule your surgery for next week."

He was almost out the door when I blurted out, "Thanks for the honesty, Doc."

Driving home, I felt peace about my decision. I knew I had taken charge, asked the right questions, and done my homework. After considering all the professional opinions available, I had chosen the one I felt was right for me.

It was Thanksgiving week when I checked into the same hospital where I had spent so much time with my dying husband. Nurses greeted me by name, and I asked about their kids and work problems. We were already well acquainted. As they prepared me for surgery, I felt strangely calm and very grateful for Dr. Lincoln Snyder, a cautious and conservative surgeon who simply removed the mass and the sentinel node and determined that the cancer had not spread into my lymph system. Praise God, I thought! Only recovery lay ahead of me now. (See Cancer Appendix on page 223 for more information.)

A few mornings after surgery, grief unexpectedly shook me again. For an entire week I was supposed to protect my stitches, keeping them dry and clean. So tough to do one-handed! I struggled to cover the wounds with gauze, then wrap myself in plastic so I could shower. That's when I broke down.

Frustrated and lonely, I let the tears flow freely. Where was Hal when I needed him most? I simply couldn't keep asking friends to stay overnight and help me tend to my wounds. I needed the comforting arms of my husband. And I was mad at myself for being a wimp. When you are independent, as I have been, it's so hard to ask for help and support. It makes you feel so vulnerable, and I wanted no part of that. I wanted to handle it alone, but I wasn't pulling it off very well.

Ho, Ho, Ho . . . Boo, Hoo, Hoo!

To make matters worse, it was now the Christmas season. My very favorite time of year! A time to be jolly! Ho, ho, ho and deck the halls! The season of joy! Why, then, did I feel like crying all the time?

Looking at the ornaments on my tree was like rubbing salt into my wounded heart. Nostalgia flooded over me as I remembered buying each one with Hal, and so many of them had sentimental significance. Hal's Santa suit hung limp and useless in the closet, and there were no holiday party invitations in my mail that season. (When Hal was alive, sometimes we had to juggle our schedules so we could make it to two parties a night.) This year folks were not quite sure what to do with me at a party! Who wants a fifth wheel, anyway? So I endured yet another loss—of the holiday traditions I had enjoyed so much that would never be the same again.

Let the Battle Begin

For me, the highlight of the season was not caroling, shopping, or baking. It was "mapping," the preliminary procedure of pinpointing the precise location of the cancer and drawing a diagram on my chest so it could be bombarded again and again by radiation. Against the oncologist's advice, I had opted not to have chemotherapy, in which both good cells and bad cells would be damaged. Radiation was less damaging, and cells would recover more easily. I was scheduled to have thirty-six radiation treatments altogether, five days per week for a little over seven weeks. Bah, humbug! I didn't want to volunteer for this.

God must have heard my subconscious cry for His direction. As I listened to my favorite gospel vocal group, The Martins, these lyrics jumped out at me:

> There's not a victory without a fight;
> There's not a sunrise without a night.
> There's not a purchase without a cost;
> There's not a Crown without a Cross.[1]

It was like God talking directly to me, preparing me for the inevitable. I knew the treatments would be a cross for me. Did I want to bear that cross? Why should I fight so desperately to hang on to life in this world? As I prayed about this, I sensed the Lord asking me a question.

"Lee, do you *want* to live?"

Meekly, I answered, "Lord, what difference does it make?"

"That's up to you, my child."

Something clicked during that conversation with the King. I got up and made the phone call to schedule the start of radiation the very next day. Every day I faithfully showed up for my treatments, canceling all speaking engagements and many other obligations. I was a model patient, so I couldn't understand why thirteen treatments later I was experiencing more pronounced side effects rather than diminished ones. My white blood cell count was down, and I was very burned and blistered from the radiation. I grew desperately weary of the humiliation involved in lying uncovered on a slab, listening to young technicians chat about dirt-biking over the weekend.

Occasionally I would realize that what I was experiencing was only a speck compared to the humiliation and pain Jesus endured when He bore *His* cross. It didn't end my suffering, but in a sense it deepened my intimacy with Him. And when I was able to remember that the ultimate outcome for Him was resurrection, I was strengthened and greatly comforted. It helped me hold on to my determination to do my part. Each time the technicians retreated behind their protective lead walls, I'd go to work. The machine would begin to move around me, grinding and beeping like a robot. I would open my spirit to any good it could bring to my ailing body and rebuke any evil effects of the treatments.

Still there were side effects—gum disease and thyroid damage. My salivary glands were damaged, making it hard for me to swallow. "I didn't see this in your brochure," I complained to the radiological oncologist. He didn't seem to understand why I was disgruntled by his prediction that these unpleasant complications should last for only two years or so.

The treatments dragged out through the Christmas season, making it anything but jolly for me. I had little energy for shopping or decorating, but I did indulge myself in one personal purchase. Hal and I had fallen in love with a painting titled *The Bridge of Faith* by Thomas Kinkade. It was expensive, and I had talked Hal out of buying it at least three times. But if ever there was a time to splurge, it was now. As I placed it over our fireplace, I reminded myself that my faith in Jesus was like the bridge in that painting. Whenever I felt weak or weary, I would come and sit in the darkened den, with a light illuminating the painting. It would soothe my soul!

As Christmas approached, I resolved to keep things as normal as possible. And having my family gather around me for the holidays proved to be a healing balm. Once again, God worked all things together for good, just as He promises.

NEW YEAR, NEW HOPE

As the year drew to a close, God gave me a beautiful gift that lifted my spirits and helped give me a new hope for the future. Reverend Jim Swanson, Hal's dear friend, came to my house, along with my closest friends, and formally ordained me as a minister. I was reminded that the most effective ministers are those who have learned to be ministered to. With that in mind, I decided I'd check into a cancer support group.

As I walked into my first session, I looked around at my fellow warriors. They were wearing scarves and wigs, some even brandishing the baldness that is a trademark of cancer therapy. Something puzzling happened. Walking in and seeing all of those suffering soldiers overwhelmed me, and I panicked. I did not feel supported there. Terror struck my heart as I listened to their stories of cancer that was spreading, of their battles, year after year. Survival had become the sole focus of their lives.

One shared a startling statistic that the equivalent of four jumbo jet loads of Americans die every day from cancer. Wow! Suddenly it hit me that I was embroiled in a life-and-death struggle. I observed that having cancer can be a catalyst for emotional and psychological growth and also an incentive for evaluating my priorities. In the support group, we talked about the fact that "with cancer patients, tissue is not the issue. It's not about cells or treatments either, it's about survival and quality of life." I thought about my mortality and pondered if my time was up. I certainly did not feel I had finished my work here on earth, but neither had Hal.

VICTIM OR VICTOR?

I decided to stick with the support group and continue to wrestle. As I did, gradually my perspective began to change from "victimized" to "victorious." As my friend Sue Buchanan summed it up in her book *I'm Alive and the Doctor's Dead:*

> Having cancer and going through a year of treatment may not have been a *privilege*, and I wouldn't wish it to happen to anyone else, but it makes me stop and ask, "Why *not*

me?" My perspective has changed on almost everything: family, friendships, reunions and my Christian faith.[2]

Sue's personal observation underscores what the Chinese seem to know innately. David Spiegel analyzes the Chinese word for cancer this way: "Cancer is a crisis in the true meaning of [the word] in Chinese . . . which is composed of two characters, one meaning danger and the other, opportunity."[3]

When cancer hits, suddenly danger becomes a daily part of life. Also comes the opportunity to face that danger with courage, determination, and even a sense of humor and thereby become a victor, no matter what the ultimate outcome.

Humorist Erma Bombeck was diagnosed with breast cancer back in 1992. Then within a short time she learned she also had adult polycystic kidney disease. She battled these conditions for four years until 1996, when she passed away from complications in the aftermath of a kidney transplant. About cancer Erma wrote: "I was hearing, 'We interrupt this life to bring you cancer.'" Yes, her life was interrupted, indeed disrupted and tragically cut short by the "C" word. But she was still a victor because she continued to use her gift of humor until the end of her life to bring laughter into people's lives. Once she even advised, "When life gives you lemons . . . stuff them in your bra!"[4]

MERRY MEDICINE

Once in a while, Hollywood really comes up with a hidden treasure. That's what I thought about the movie *Patch Adams*. It was based on a true story about a medical student who had genuine compassion for patients, unlike many of the doctors he observed. Patch grew to believe that humor and warmth and even some radical departure from normal medical protocol could enhance the healing process in patients who are confined in the hospital. He could often be found wearing a red clown nose and cheering patients with outrageous antics that made them laugh. As you might guess, the more staid, conservative members of the medical community were outraged by Patch Adams's "merry medicine," so they held a hearing to get him expelled. At this hearing, Patch made a soul-searching speech that went like this:

> Is not a doctor someone who helps someone else? When did the term doctor gain such spiritual reverence? When did a doctor become more than a trusted and learned friend who visited and treated the ill? And if a patient dies, what's wrong with dying? Why can't doctors treat death with a certain amount of humanity and decency and, God forbid, maybe even humor? Death is not the enemy of medical practice. Let's fight the disease of indifference. I have sat in medical school and heard lectures on professional distance from patients. A doctor's mission should not just be to prevent death, but to improve life. That's why if you treat a disease you may lose, but if you treat a human being you will win, no matter what the outcome.

Sounds like a "God idea" to me! In fact, the Bible even talks about laughter as being the best kind of medicine, so I have a feeling that Patch Adams stole this idea from the Master Physician Himself. It may seem silly, but watching that movie was a turning point for me because it prompted me to change my focus from "how can I get through this trial?" to "how can I help others through their trials?"

Inspired by the example of Patch Adams, I gathered together a team of friends—magicians, a cowboy, a face painter, and a ventriloquist with a dummy named Ezra. This was a God-project! I was sure of it.

The next week our troupe went to a large children's hospital. We visited children in several oncology wards—kids who were pale and sick, in different stages of treatment. Many were confined to wheelchairs or dragging IV towers around behind them. The children ranged in age from two to fifteen in this hospital, which is well-known for groundbreaking work in bone marrow transplants for kids with cancer.

As I moved among these sick little ones, I wore a homemade clown costume with quiltlike patches all over it and, of course, a big red nose. The nurse took me from room to room to see the boys and girls who were too sick to get out of bed. Talk about tugging at your heartstrings! Here I was, a strong, adult woman fighting this demon called cancer, and here were these little children also caught in its grip.

When I visited with the older kids, I'd let them know I was in the same boat with them. "You have cancer too?" asked one teenager. The camaraderie was cool!

This day was therapy for me—as much as any amount of radiation and chemicals. How wonderful to hear these children giggle as they watched the magicians, enjoyed rope tricks by Cowboy Regis, had their faces painted by Debbie with stars and rainbows, and were entertained by Gail with her ventriloquism. I passed out joke gifts, "smiles-on-a-stick," and, yes, even red clown noses.

It was a joy! And for the first time in a long time I really felt I had found that solid rock to sink my feet into again. The dreaded "C" word or any other of life's aftershocks couldn't defeat me as long as I rested on God's foundation. Healing was, after all, a process that took time. It also took making a deliberate choice to take charge of my illness and be victor over it. As Patch Adams said . . . no matter what the outcome.

SORTING THINGS OUT

Let's take a moment to identify a few helpful principles from what we've seen in this chapter. Plant these principles like "red flags" in your mental data bank, and you can call them up when you need them in the future.

Red Flag #1: There is no quota for suffering. Aftershocks may occur all throughout your life.

Red Flag #2: Be a victor rather than a victim. When going through a medical crisis, or any other type of crisis, be proactive. Ask questions and seek out as many professional opinions as you need to help you make a decision you feel peaceful about.

Red Flag #3: When faced with a cross to bear, you do have a choice. Before choosing not to take it up, remember that Jesus took up His cross for your sake. Is God asking you to bear a cross now for His sake?

Red Flag #4: Every dangerous place in life is also a place of opportunity. Don't let fear of danger blind you to the opportunities.

Red Flag #5: The "way of escape" through trials often can be found in looking for ways to reach out to others. Look for ways to lighten the load of others, and you'll likely find yourself lightening up!

🌿 ASKING . . . AND ACTING!

STEP 1: ASKING

Does submission to God mean we must suffer in silence, without ever questioning or admitting anger or frustration? Can there be true intimacy with Him without unbridled honesty?

STEP 2: ACTING

Whether the battle you are fighting is over your health, finances, or a broken heart, a loss of any kind can leave you feeling shaky. Don't give in to it! Fight that thing by making the following into a sign for your fridge or bathroom mirror, only replace the word "cancer" with whatever you are battling.

> **What (Cancer) Cannot Do**
> (Cancer) is so limited . . .
> It cannot cripple love.
> It cannot shatter hope.
> It cannot corrode faith.
> It cannot destroy peace.
> It cannot kill friendship.
> It cannot suppress memories.
> It cannot silence courage.
> It cannot invade the soul.
> It cannot steal eternal life.
> It cannot conquer the spirit.

TEN

THE ROLLER COASTER OF LIFE

Why are you so downcast, O my soul?
Why so disturbed within me?
Put your hope in God,
for I will yet praise him,
my Savior and my God.

Psalm 42:5

Up.
  Down.
  Up.
  Down.
  My life had become a series of drastic ups and downs. As much as I tried to stay up, I often found myself spiraling downward, and I didn't always know why.

Sometimes, when I had a down day, I figured it was due to my raging hormones, now that I was on hormone blocker medication. My confusion could have been caused by complications from my treatments. A medication overdose? Just missing my husband? Who knows?

One of the worst down times I experienced had a definite cause. It came when my oncologist told me that an X ray had revealed cysts on an ovary. He couldn't say for sure if they were cancerous, but he had even gone so far as to schedule me for surgery. He had also made an appointment for later that day with a gynecological oncologist. Obviously, he believed that whatever was going on in my ovaries wasn't anything to fool around with.

This wasn't exactly my idea of a good way to start the day. I was already running late for my haircut appointment. After that, I had my radiation treatment, which always zapped me of my strength. And then the appointment with the new doctor.

SEEKING SUPPORT

Somehow, during this hectic day, I found myself with an hour to spare at the cancer center and dropped in on a support group meeting. Here I was in the War Room again, surrounded by fellow soldiers. I was asked to share my story.

I didn't want to tell them about Hal—it wouldn't exactly encourage them—so I told them instead about my surgery for breast cancer. The woman sitting next to me reached out and patted me on the hand. "Yes, that was my first cancer too," she said sympathetically.

I should have bolted right then, but I stayed anyway. And I compounded that mistake by mentioning that I was undergoing radiation treatments.

"But . . . but . . . didn't your doctor recommend chemotherapy first?" one woman sputtered.

"Yes," I replied, "but I refused chemo."

That was the wrong thing to say. The room went deathly quiet. But the faces surrounding me spoke volumes. Many of these women were obviously suffering terribly from chemotherapy and were struggling to get to the end of it. Who did I think I was to avoid chemo altogether?

I should have left well enough alone. Instead, I kept on talking. I told them they were looking at some cysts on an ovary, but I was sure it wasn't any big deal and that I'd be back on my feet in a few days.

The silence seemed to grow deeper. And then the barrage of questions came. How many cysts? Where were they? How many centimeters? And on and on. These women were trying to get me to face the reality that I was probably dealing with a recurrence of cancer, something many of them had endured.

A feisty gal sitting across the table from me obviously thought I was a dreamer. "Are you aware of how common it is for breast cancer to metastasize to either the ovaries or the uterus? The odds are against you."

My heart was in my throat, and I quickly glanced at my watch and said I had to leave for my appointment with the gynecological oncologist. My head was spinning.

Fortunately for me, I liked Dr. Jeb Brown right away. He was young, but he had an excellent reputation—I'd already checked it out—and he mentioned that he'd seen *Patch Adams* and thought it gave an accurate portrayal of much of the medical profession. That made him A-OK in my book. I could tell right away that he had no delusions of grandeur and didn't consider himself to be godlike—as opposed to some other doctors I had encountered.

After (another) pelvic exam (ugh!) and a look at my records, he asked me what I expected. I told him I would expect that he'd make three small incisions, take out the cysts, and then I'd return to my speaking schedule in a few days.

Dr. Brown smiled, shook his head, and explained that because the cysts might be malignant, he could not risk trying to squeeze them out of a small laparoscopic opening. If he did, they could rupture and the cancer might spread. He tactfully explained that a woman my age (watch it, buster!) and with my history had no need of any female organs that might become cancerous in the future. What he was getting at was that he needed to perform a full hysterectomy on me, "the old fashioned way," complete with a big incision and a six- to eight-week recovery.

That was the good news.

Now came the bad news.

If the cysts were cancerous, the incision would be bigger, and much more of the area would be explored, excised, and scraped, including taking out any more "questionable-appearing parts" from my bowels. I felt like I was going to pass out.

But he wasn't through. The surgery, which had originally been scheduled as an outpatient procedure, would have to be moved to the hospital's main operating room in case complications should arise.

It's strange, but the worst part of all this, for me, was that it wreaked havoc with my speaking schedule. My itinerary was completely full. I'd have to cancel more meetings, and I'd have to do it on short notice. Tickets had already been sold, advertising paid for, and I hated to let people down. But what else could I do? Of course, this also meant that I'd have to return deposits for speaking engagements (which I'd already spent) and try to find a way to survive through several more weeks without an income.

THE DAM BREAKS

As I closed the door of my van in the hospital parking lot, I felt something stirring within me. All the way home, my emotions crashed over me like a tidal wave. I had such a deep sense of needing Hal. I felt as if everything I had been through during the last few months had suddenly come crashing back down on me. I could barely see the road ahead of me through the hysterical tears that flooded my eyes.

I grabbed for my car phone to make a spiritual 911 call. Thankfully, my prayer partner Janice was at home. I was crying so hard she didn't recognize my voice at first. I gasped out that I needed her right away, and she said she'd meet me at my house. She got there about the same time I did, bringing another friend, Pat, with her.

I felt I had caught an emotional tidal wave that could crash me on a shore I'd never landed on before.

The two of them helped me out of my van as I sobbed that I might have ovarian cancer and was scheduled for a full hysterectomy, and who knew what else? I had never before experienced such overwhelming feelings of grief and disappointment, and that is saying an awful lot.

They finally managed to get me into the house, where I crashed onto the den floor, sobbing and crying out to the Lord.

"God! I need Hal right now! I can't go through this next one without him! Why am I alone at a time like this? I cannot handle having another cancer! It's much too soon!"

Then I began to question Him: "When will this come to an end? Am I being tested? Am I flunking? What's wrong?"

I felt as if I had been jilted by God.

I know my dear friends were scared half out of their minds by my frantic display. They were on either side of me, holding on as if they were keeping me from falling over the edge of a cliff, and they were praying. (It's a wonder they didn't call 911. I know it must have looked like I was cracking up!) It was a terrible scene, but if I could see it from this vantage point, I'd probably get a good chuckle. On one side of me, my dear Episcopalian friend was crying out to God for "mercy." On the other side, my psychologist friend was saying, "Yes, God, we admit that we are very angry with you. We face it."

Angry?

I was beyond anger! I had come to the very end of myself. I lashed out at God as I pounded my fist on the coffee table. "So where is the God of Elijah?"

"Where's the God Who promises I'll never have more sorrow than I can take?"

"Where's the Miracle Worker I've believed in?"

"You said You'd be a 'defender of the widow!' Now's the time to step up to the plate!"

On and on I went, releasing my doubts and the bitterness and betrayal I felt I had received from the God I served— the One I knew could help me, if only He wanted to!

I found myself raising my hand, reaching out for Hal, but then remembered that he was gone. I pulled back my arm: "No, I can't have him! He can't help me. You took him!"

After nearly two hours of this, my anger was spent, and my tone suddenly changed. "Lee," I said out loud, "get a grip now. God took Hal off this planet, and he is unreachable now. Jesus is your only connection to the other world. God, I accept Your will. Holy Spirit, rescue me from this pit! You are a good God!" At last, the truth was coming through.

Suddenly, I noticed I was quoting Scripture to myself:

"You are my refuge and my strength."

"You said the plans You have for me are for good and not for evil."

"You said, 'No man plucks them out of My hand,' so I'm still in Your hand."

"You said, 'Come unto Me all ye who are heavy laden.' Well, here I am."

"You said You would never leave me or forsake me."

I continued quoting Scriptures that I had learned long ago and thought I'd forgotten. But now, in this time of crisis, God's Word was bubbling up in me. And the more I quoted, the more I settled down.

Now, what happened next may sound odd, but it is absolutely true, and I'll never forget it. My body began to shake and tingle. I mean really shake!

I was shouting to my friends, "Touch me! Can you feel it? It's the Spirit of God!" They said they couldn't feel anything from the outside, but on the inside I felt as if they'd hauled me over to the electric switch and plugged me into the outlet. In the midst of this, I heard my friends discussing what they should do to help me.

"No! Let it be! It's Him!" I commanded.

Finally, after about ten minutes, the shaking subsided.

I lay limp on the floor, wrung out like a woman who had just given birth. The sweet Holy Spirit had swooped down on me, pulling me through the eye of the needle. What had I experienced? Was it physical healing? Or was it simply a restoration and a rebuilding of my faith? Whatever it was, it was fantastic.

After my friends brewed a pot of tea, they remarked that they'd never seen anything like that before. Me neither. When they left, I crawled up the stairs and fell into bed and into the most contented sleep I'd had in months.

$\frac{Q_{l}}{Q_{l}}$

Disappointment with God is a process in which the soul can be torn apart and patched together again.

PREPARING FOR HEAVEN

When I awoke, refreshed in the morning, I began to think that God was preparing to take me home. I had hoped and prayed so hard for Hal's healing, which hadn't come, so why should I think the Lord had chosen to heal me? I was tired of fighting and didn't have much fight left in me anyhow! I remembered the little boy's prayer, overheard by his mother:

> Now I lay me down to rest,
> and hope to pass tomorrow's test.
> But if I should die before I wake,
> that's one less test I'll have to take!

Not telling anyone what I was doing, I feverishly began cleaning out my garage. I didn't want my family to have to go through that mess after I was gone. I tossed out all my old high school and college memories. I emptied files that I hadn't looked at in years. And once the garage had been taken care of, I tackled the closets. I wanted to be prepared to go to heaven.

PATCH GOES TO SURGERY

When the morning for my surgery arrived, my friends met me in the chapel and we prayed together. What a comfort that was! I had perfect peace, even though I was secretly prepared to hear the worst. I had a supply of red noses to pass out to keep things light, and the staff loved it. I had also asked my artist pal, Debbie, to help me give a message to my surgeons. What fun we had drawing maps and writing funny instructions all over my belly! And what a surprise the surgeons got!

As I lay on the gurney, rumbling down the hall toward the operating room, I kept a few red noses under my arm. We stopped in the hall outside the OR and waited for over an hour.

"What's the delay?" I asked. "I'm getting cold."

"It's an emergency," the nurse replied.

"What kind of emergency?" I asked.

She leaned over and whispered in my ear, "Harvesting." I had no idea what she meant.

Just then, the doors burst open and two gurneys rolled past with teenage boys on them. It was then that I understood what "harvesting" meant. One of the boys seemed to be hanging on to life. The other was dead—his organs were to be transplanted into the other youth.

"Oh, Lord," I prayed, "help me keep my petty problems in perspective."

During my wait for surgery, I began talking to the anesthesiologist. Of course, he got a clown nose. I asked to speak to my surgeon again, and when he came in his green scrubs, I gave him one of the noses and said, "Doc, I know what your plan is for this surgery. But you can't imagine how many folks are praying for you to have wisdom. Please be open to a different plan—one less severe than the 'big cut' you talked about. Will you be open to that?"

He patted my hand. "Now, Lee, we already know what we have to do."

I found out later that after I was under the anesthesia, Dr. Brown had put his red nose on, and then placed one on me. I was told there was an unusual lightheartedness in the operating room as they surveyed the artwork on my abdomen.

I also heard that just as the surgeon was about to do the "big cut," he remembered what I had asked him, called for the laproscopic equipment, and said, "I'll just try it." When he peeked inside, it appeared that there was no cancer on the cysts! He was able to do a simple hysterectomy without the debilitating cutting. I was told that he remarked to the staff during the operation, "This gal does important work, so this will help her get back to it sooner."

In the recovery room, as I was in and out of consciousness I could hear the muffled, excited voices of my friends and family. Were they saying what I thought they were saying? "No cancer!"

It wasn't until 4:30 A.M. the next morning that I summoned enough courage to lift the sheet to check out my "big cut." I immediately burst into tears when I saw that there wasn't one! I was crying for joy, and then suddenly stopped.

"Then this means I'm not going to heaven?" I asked. Perplexed, I mumbled, "Then I cleaned up for nothing?" I also realized that God wasn't through with me yet and that I had to do everything I could to make sure my last years were greater than my former years.

As I thought about what I had been through, I realized that I had discovered three important truths for anyone who is facing a serious illness or other personal tragedy. It's important to:

- Get good and angry.
- Use positive self-talk.
- Tell yourself the truth.

Let me explain.

GET GOOD AND ANGRY

It is important to be honest with God, even when you're angry with Him. That's what had happened to me on my den floor. I had so much stress and anger welling up inside of me that I couldn't contain it.

When that happens, the Lord will never respond with, "I had no idea you were that angry," or "You're hurting my feelings. Please be more careful." In fact, God may be waiting for you to spill it out, to empty yourself of all your negative thoughts about what's happening to you. God knows you feel cheated, and He wants you to get that destructive feeling out.

If you haven't given vent to your feelings, I suggest you do so right now. If you need to beat on a pillow or scream at the top of your lungs, go ahead! Permission granted! If you try to hold the anger in, it will find a way to seep out in other ways, or it can cause damage to your body.

Major league baseball pitcher Dave Dravecky remembers how he was affected by anger. On live TV everyone saw him pitch his last ball as his shoulder dislocated again with a second bout with cancer. He says, "I didn't deal with it well—I was miserable and unpleasant to be around. I lashed out in random acts of anger that had no relation to what was happening around me."[1]

Any negative turn of events in your life can bring about the same type of resentment: finding out you have a special-needs child; the breakup of your marriage or your parents' marriage; having a friend diagnosed with AIDS. There are many similar situations that can produce anger deep inside, and that anger must be vented.

GIVE YOURSELF A GOOD TALKING TO

In many of the Psalms, including Psalm 42:5, David spends a great deal of time reminding himself of God's goodness. When David was going through a bad time—and he went through *many* bad times—he needed to remind himself that God loved him and would see him through. You and I need to do the same thing.

I've developed this habit of talking to myself—hopefully not out in public where other people could be watching me. Whenever I have an emotional or physical setback, I stop in my tracks and have a conversation with myself:

- Why are you so discouraged, O my soul?
- You have a connection with God.
- You know God will work this out for your good.
- Hasn't God been faithful to you?

As I looked back on my experience, I was amazed at how much it mirrored the experience of David as he went through the entire range of emotions in Psalm 77. At first, he was angry and confused.

> I cried out to God for help;
>   I cried out to God to hear me. . . .
> "Will the Lord reject us forever?
>   Will he never show his favor again?
> Has his unfailing love vanished forever?
>   Has his promise failed for all time?
> Has God forgotten to be merciful?"
>
> verses 1, 7–8

Then, suddenly, David began to remember the truth about God.

> I will remember the deeds of the LORD:
>   yes, I will remember your miracles of long ago.
> I will meditate on all your works
>   and consider all your mighty deeds.
> Your ways, O God, are holy.
>   What god is so great as our God?
>
> verses 11–13

When I remind myself of what God has done for me, and when I hear others tell of what God has done for them, I am encouraged. I don't know what you're going through, but I do know that God is real, that He loves you, and, that if you cling to Him, He will see you through.

When actor George Burns played the role of God in the movie *Oh, God!* I had to chuckle. A lot of the dialogue was way off base (according to Scripture), but there was also a lot to think about. Even when God appeared in a court of law, people still refused to believe in Him. He remarked, "You don't believe in me? What about the devil—from that Hollywood movie? Nobody had a problem believing the devil lived in that girl. All she had to do was wet the rug, throw up some pea soup, and everybody believed. So in the devil you can believe, but not in God?"

Tell Yourself the Truth

It's also important to rehearse out loud what you know as truth.

Truths about God.

- God is love.
- He has not forgotten you.
- He wants to help you through this.
- He did not cause the suffering in your life.

Truths about your current situation.

- What you are going through is no surprise to God.
- God will use this experience for your ultimate good.
- This too shall pass.

Truths about you.

- God still loves you.
- You will recover, with God's help.
- Though you may feel lost right now, God will show you the way back.
- You can walk through any valley with the Good Shepherd by your side.

When you tell yourself the truth, you are building your faith and preparing your heart to receive a blessing from God. You are doing what the prophet Elisha told God's people to do in the desert—namely, dig ditches by faith to receive the water God would supply. (You can find the story in 2 Kings 3.)

I urge you to keep your eyes on God and be prepared for showers of blessings, even if you don't see the slightest hint of a rain cloud on the horizon.

- Remember that God is the rainmaker.
- Though you may feel stranded in the desert right now, carve a ditch with your faith and wait for a supernatural God to make His presence known.
- God's love will fill your ditch; He will not let you go dry.

George Matheson's old hymn "Oh Love That Wilt Not Let Me Go" says it so well:

> Oh Joy that seekest me through pain,
> I cannot close my heart to Thee;
> I trace the rainbow through the rain,
> And feel the promise is not vain
> That morn shall tearless be.

NO PROMISES

Finally, after what seemed like forever, I completed my cycle of radiation treatments. I was anxious to see the radiation oncologist for the last time. I wanted him to pat me on the back and tell me I was going to be fine. But he didn't.

Instead, he peered at me over the top of his glasses and said, "I'm sorry, Mrs. Ezell, but I can't give you the assurance you seek. I prescribed seven weeks of five-day-a-week therapy for you, but you had another plan. You took a few days off here and there to go speak in Denver and Dallas. So, really, you didn't follow my instructions and I cannot give you any reassurances." He seemed to be like Pilate, washing his hands of any responsibility for my situation.

My regular oncologist was just as discouraging. He chastised me for rejecting chemotherapy and for using vitamins and herbal supplements which he, apparently, did not approve of. "I'm writing in your file that you rejected my recommendations," he said.

Good night! What happened to the days when you went to the family doctor not only for treatment but also for some comfort and encouragement that you were doing well?

I tearfully walked to my car, sat there, and told the Lord I'd decided to get my comfort and support from a Higher Power—the Spirit of God within me. I wondered if my doctors were so afraid of a malpractice suit that they would refuse to give any patient a commitment of wellness. As I prayed, the peace returned. I realized that in the months ahead I would have to continue to live by faith and not by sight.

The threat of cancer's return would always be dangling over my head. But the Lord was with me.

Now that's blessed assurance.

🌿 ASKING . . . AND ACTING!

STEP 1: ASKING

What do you think the Bible means when it says, "We live by faith, not by sight" (2 Cor. 5:7)? Does this seem unfair sometimes? How does this Scripture apply to your current situation?

STEP 2: ACTING

If someone you loved was terribly angry with you, you could not take steps toward reconciliation until that person admitted the angry feelings. Although God is omniscient and knows our thoughts and feelings even better than we do, He also respects our privacy. Are you angry with God for any reason today? If so, He may be waiting for you to tell Him so before He takes steps toward healing the breach. Why not sit down and write Him a letter? Pour your heart into the words you write, laying them out before Him with complete honesty. Seal your letter in an envelope and place it in your Bible. Then pray earnestly that He will "read" it and respond to your desperate hurting. As for you, now it's time to get quiet and listen! Reconciliation takes time, but ultimately it can deepen your relationship with God.

FOR BIBLE STUDY

2 Kings 3
Psalms 42:5; 77:1, 7–8, 11–13

ELEVEN

FAITH TAKES TIME

I know God can heal all things . . .
broken lives and broken wings.
Only He can mend a heart
that time has torn apart.
As the seasons make their turn
there's a lesson to be learned.
Broken wings take time to mend
before I learn to fly again.

Disappointment?

Yes, I'm well acquainted with it.

Perhaps you are too.

When you think of your anguished times of disillusionment, perhaps you (like me) were staking everything on God coming through for you—with what you wanted. Perhaps you were hoping for recovery from disease, the return of a prodigal child, the restoration of a marriage, or restitution from a friend who had betrayed you (perhaps even a friend from church). But instead, the disease progressed and the patient died, the prodigal child is still out there, there has been no improvement in your marriage, or the friend who betrayed you feels no repercussions or pangs of guilt for what she did.

If so, you know how I was feeling after Hal died, and when the doctor would give me no reassurance for my own recovery.

I felt helpless. Totally dependent upon God for my survival. Most of the time, that was enough.

But sometimes I wanted more. I wanted assurances that I was going to be fine—assurances my doctors would not give.

To make matters worse, I felt that my grief and trials had become the subject of much speculation on the part of people who knew me—or who, at least, knew my ministry. I felt that some were watching me—with curiosity more than compassion—waiting to see if God was going to come through for me.

Perhaps you know the feeling. If so, you're in some good company. Remember how people taunted our Lord as He hung on the cross: "He saved others, now let's see if He can save Himself" (see Matt. 27:42). And, "He's calling for Elijah. Let's see if Elijah comes to help Him!"

Perhaps you too feel that you are hanging out there with no miracle on the horizon.

If so, I want you to know that you can and will survive! God does care, and He will not leave you to tumble in the wind forever. As Jesus said, "I will not leave you as orphans" (John 14:18).

But I have discovered that God deals in love more often than He deals in miraculous displays of His power. In the end, there is nothing more miraculous than His love for you, and it is that love that will prevail against all odds and bring you the resurrection you have sought for so long!

As I dealt with sorrow and fear—first through the loss of my cherished husband and then through my own battle with cancer—I discovered that my progress toward spiritual wholeness and health was anything but rapid!

I've heard grief described as a process in which one thousand candles are lit. As you go through the grieving process, you blow out a few candles at a time. Perhaps you've extinguished a hundred or so of those candles—maybe even made your way through six or seven hundred of them. But then, all of a sudden and seemingly out of nowhere, a spark sets them all on fire again, and you're right back where you were before you started blowing them out in the first place.

In my head, I knew my body was the temple of the Holy Spirit. But I felt it had been bombed out. So many things I cherished had been damaged that I needed repairs spiritually, emotionally, and physically. Because I felt I had misinterpreted God, I was afraid of what might lie ahead. I was praying every day that God would begin the restoration process in my life.

I discovered that the journey from grief back to faith takes time. How much time? As much time as it takes. I know that sounds flippant, but it's also true. No one can say for sure how long it will take you to overcome a tragedy that has taken place in your life. Everybody is different. But no one can simply "bounce back" from a devastating loss without his or her faith suffering some damage. At least, that is the conclusion I have come to through talking to dozens of men and women who have gone through a time of suffering and grief.

If you are trying to find your way back to the comfortable world you used to know before tragedy overtook you, here are some things that will help along the way.

1. Everyone has a cross to carry.
2. Burying your grief and sorrow is not the same as dealing with them.
3. It's all right to become angry with God, but you've got to get over it and forgive Him.
4. It's okay to wrestle with God.

5. It's true that misery loves company, so share your difficult times with people who care about you.
6. There's no need to sign up for a guilt trip.
7. You don't have to be a victim.

Let's start at the top.

EVERYONE HAS A CROSS TO CARRY

If you're old enough, you may recall the words to the old hymn we used to sing:

> Must Jesus bear the cross alone,
> And all the world go free?
> No, there's a cross for everyone,
> And there's a cross for me.

I haven't heard anyone sing that song in years. And that's regrettable. Maybe we Christians would do a better job of dealing with life's difficulties if we understood that verse. It would help us remember that Jesus told those who wanted to be His followers that they must "take up his cross daily" (Luke 9:23). He also told us that "in this world you will have trouble" (John 16:33).

When you're going through something terrible—like the terminal illness or death of someone you love, or a diagnosis of a life-threatening disease like cancer—it's easy to start thinking you've been singled out for some reason. You see other people laughing and having a good time, and you wonder why they're having so much fun when you're barely making it through the day.

But you know what? Everyone has a cross to carry. Everyone has to go through a "dark night of the soul."

Whatever you are going through, it may help to consider the experience to be a cross you have to bear—just as our Lord carried His own heavy cross to Calvary. There was no miracle waiting for Christ when He reached the top of that hill. But because He went through that terrible ordeal, He understands what it's like to suffer, and He feels our pain deeply.

I imagine that as our Messiah went through His last few days before the crucifixion, He experienced the same confusing and frightening thoughts that go through our minds when we're in distress. I think about how He must have felt in the Garden of Gethsemane when He asked the Father to "take this cup from me." I wonder what thoughts crossed His mind when Herod taunted Him and demanded that He perform a miracle. And I can't help but wonder if even Jesus didn't begin to doubt the Father's love as He hung on the cross watching those He was dying for dance around and mock Him in His agony.

Dietrich Bonhoeffer, a young German pastor, was executed during World War II after being convicted of his part in a plot to overthrow Adolf Hitler's Nazi regime. As he sat in prison in emotional agony, knowing that each day could be his last, he scribbled these words on a notepad: "Only the suffering God can help."[1]

How true! Only a God who understands what it's like to toss and turn all night long, unable to sleep because life has become so unbearable, can understand how to comfort us and bring us safely through to the other side of the difficulty.

It was a startling thing for me when I came to realize that God was walking alongside me in my time of loss and sorrow. He wasn't going to speak some "bibbity-bobbity-boo" and make it all better for me, because He wanted me to grow and mature through the experience of carrying my own cross. At the same time, He was there to help me carry that cross, to empathize with me, to weep with me, and to whisper that He loves me and that there will, indeed, be a happy ending, no matter how dark things are right now.

BURYING YOUR GRIEF DOESN'T WORK

Another important thing I've learned as I've made my way through the grieving process is that burying your grief and sorrow is not the same as dealing with them.

I tried to bury my grief and it didn't work. I found out that what I was doing was a lot like stuffing one of those spring-filled rubber snakes into a can. Sooner or later, that lid's going to come off. When it does, that snake is going to jump out and you're right back to square one.

If you try to bury your grief, it is bound to manifest itself in other ways—including anxiety, anger, and even physical illness. The only beneficial way to deal with grief is to meet it head on, to face your feelings, to recognize that it's perfectly normal for you to feel this way, and that it may be months before things even begin to feel stable again.

I went through having to talk myself out of bed on mornings when I didn't have speaking engagements. I'd start to get out of bed, decide I couldn't face the day, and retreat back underneath the covers, reaching out to Hal's side of the bed.

I had to force myself to choose the path of acceptance. I had to accept that Hal was gone, and I had to accept that my life had to continue, that God had things He still wanted me to do.

It was no "yellow brick road," because acceptance meant facing some hard realities and dealing with some issues I didn't really want to face. I often relied on one particular Scripture to get me going in the morning, and that was Deuteronomy 30:19–20: "I have set before you life and death. . . . Now choose life . . . that you may love the LORD your God, listen to his voice, and hold fast to him. For the LORD is your life."

Sometimes before I could summon up enough strength to put my feet on the floor in the morning, I could faintly hear the Lord asking me, "Do you want to be well?" It was important for me to acknowledge that, "Yes, Lord, I do want to be well," so He could give me His divine direction. I did not want to be counted among those who wouldn't answer the question because they had lost hope and felt that there was no way they could ever feel whole again.

After actor William Shatner lost his wife in a swimming-pool accident, he made this insightful statement in an interview with CBS news: "Grief is like having your leg cut off—you don't know how it happened or where it went, and you have the phantom feeling that it is still there."

In the new movie version of the Broadway hit production *The King and I*, Anna was depicted as a grieving widow who couldn't let go of the man she had lost. The Buddhist king (who believed he had many lives to live) challenged Anna by asking her if it was true that, as a Christian, she felt that she had only one life to live. When she answered his question with a meek "yes," the king replied, "Then it seems you'd better get on with it." It was a tearful and poignant reminder for me.

My grief was natural and right, as long as I did not allow it to consume me. In 1 Thessalonians 4:13, the Bible reminds us that we are not to grieve as those who have no hope. Life may not play out like a Disney movie, but there will be a happy ending for those who love God. For the Christian, our story doesn't end with tears and unbearable sadness but with genuine contentment and legitimate joy.

IT'S ALL RIGHT TO FEEL ANGRY WITH GOD

Why pretend you're not angry with God if you really are? He knows it anyway, and I've discovered that He can take it! Although you feel angry with God, you've got to get over it and forgive Him.

If you are passing through a time of grief, it is very important that you deal honestly with your anger and your doubts about God's mercy. After all, you are not alone in your pain or your doubts. Even King David, whom the Bible describes as "a man after God's own heart," had his times of doubting. He wrote, "But as for me, my feet had almost slipped; I had nearly lost my foothold. For I envied the arrogant when I saw the prosperity of the wicked" (Ps. 73:2–3).

How often I could identify with those words as I dealt with my anger and grief. I was sliding back down to a place I didn't want to see again, and I couldn't seem to find a solid foothold to stop me. In this passage, David is giving voice to a question that torments all of us at one time or another. If God is good, then He would certainly be good to His children. But if that's true, why does it seem that so often His children suffer, while people who don't give a rip about God sail through life unscathed?

Such doubts, which are especially strong when someone is in the middle of the turmoil of grief, are totally normal and understandable. Jesus never showed displeasure over doubting questions asked honestly.

When the man who will be forever known as "Doubting Thomas" (poor guy) said he refused to believe that Jesus was risen from the dead unless "I see the nail marks in his hands and put my finger where the nails were" (John 20:25), Jesus didn't rebuke him. Rather, the Lord revealed Himself to Thomas and exhorted him with the words, "Blessed are those who have not seen and yet have believed" (v. 29). That's us! We can't see anything convincing right now, but let's believe anyhow.

When Christ's cousin, John the Baptist, baptized Jesus, he publicly declared him to be "the Lamb of God, who takes away the sin of the world" (John 1:29). But later on, after John was thrown into prison by Herod, he began to doubt and actually sent messengers to Jesus to ask Him, "Are you the one? Or should we look for another?" When Jesus received that doubting message from John, His gentle reply was that they should go back and report to John all the wonders they had seen—the sick being healed, the dead being raised, and so on. All of these things gave silent testimony to the fact that Jesus was indeed the Messiah, "the Lamb of God." Similarly, when we look around us, we see hundreds of people who are ready to testify about the wonderful things God has done in their lives. They have been healed from sickness and delivered from addiction. Their unbearable sorrow has been transformed into unspeakable joy! Yes, God is at work in the world, and the evidence is all around us.

It is hard in these times to have faith. Perhaps if we had faith, we could change the times.

I also believe there is another answer to the question, "Why does God let His children suffer while the bad guys seem to have an easy time of it?" God is not a prankster nor a tease. He is not an absentee landlord. He is patiently waiting for the wicked to change their ways and come to Him. But someday His patience will expire. His children will hear Him say, "Come my beloved, enter into the rest I have prepared for you," but the wicked will hear, "Depart from me, I never knew you" (see Matt. 25:31–46).

I also think it's important to keep in mind that God has His purposes for everything.

When Jesus heard that His dear friend Lazarus was deathly ill, He waited two days to go to him. God's purpose was for Jesus to raise Lazarus from the dead. But in the meantime, his family had to suffer through the excruciating loss. And didn't Lazarus have to die again later on? Of course he did. And I wonder if Mary and Martha once again called on their dear friend Jesus for help. Can't you see it?

"Hello, Peter, how's your mother-in-law? Yes, well, that's nice. Uh, guess what! Lazarus did it again. That's right. Dead as a doornail. Yeah, we think it was his heart. Well, anyway, can you get the Lord to come right away? After all, he hasn't been dead very long this time and it ought to be easier to resurrect him."

And what about Jesus' earthly father, Joseph? The Bible doesn't tell us for sure, but apparently he died when Jesus was still a very young man. If so, why didn't Jesus stop him from dying? After all, Christ knew Joseph's death would leave Mary a helpless widow (before the days of life insurance and social security). Again, God had His purposes, and we need to learn to rest in that knowledge.

One day those purposes will be made completely clear to all of us, and when that happens, we'll all get in line to get our questions answered!

But until that day comes, there will be times when God's reasons are hidden from us mere mortals, and there will be times when we become angry at God and need to forgive Him. Not for His sake, but for our own. After all, God never makes a mistake or does anything wrong, so He never needs forgiveness from anyone. But we need to forgive God if our anger is coming between Him and us and preventing us from getting as close to Him as we need to be.

If you need to forgive God, do it now. Just get down on your knees and tell Him you don't understand what's going on in your life, but you have decided to forgive Him and continue to trust Him anyway.

I remember the weekend my sweet husband Hal forgave God. We were away on a marriage retreat weekend, and it occurred to Hal that he had subconsciously been holding God responsible for the death of his two former wives.

On that marriage retreat, Hal came to realize that all these years, way down deep inside, he had blamed God for the loss of these two women. God had the power, and they had prayed and believed and done everything they knew to do to get Him to use it, but both of them had died anyway. When Hal cried this out during that marriage retreat, he came to the more logical conclusion that God was not really to be blamed. He forgave God that night and saw a real change begin to take place in his attitude.

IT'S OKAY TO WRESTLE WITH GOD

I have no delusions that I have experienced great suffering. In the eternal scheme of things, I've only had some rough times and plowed some hard ground. A biblical character I can relate well to is Jacob, because of the way he wrestled with God (see Genesis 32). Yes, I've had my nose out of joint more than once regarding my afflictions, but Jacob had his thigh out of joint in his struggle with God. I too walk differently now. I'm not as cocky as I was before. Perhaps I've been humbled by my own doubts. I walk with a kind of limp now.

If you are struggling with God, I urge you to adopt the same attitude Jacob had, an attitude that "I will not let you go until you bless me." I urge you to get a better grasp on the things of God and hold on for dear life. Believe that God will reward those who diligently seek Him.

My own reward has come in peace, in inner strength, in understanding, and in knowing something more about the loving character of God. Your reward awaits you. Don't give up; stay in the ring! Set your face like a flint to discover the things in your heart that you know are true. Your trophy will be a crown of life that no one—and no future struggle—can take from you.

Now I find it hard to trust anyone who doesn't walk with a limp. I wonder if they've ever really wrestled with God over the hard questions of life. Are they in denial? Have they just given up because they don't think there are any answers? If so, how sad.

God was not at all miffed with Jacob because Jacob wrestled with God. He was impressed. In fact, He even changed Jacob's name to Israel (with a much better meaning) and the Bible says that God blessed him there.

Can you imagine how his older brother, Esau, might have responded to the change in his brother? This conniving brother, Jacob, had cheated him out of his birthright. He had been a cocky, self-confident, "don't get in my way" sort of fellow, and now he came home walking with a limp—his permanent trophy of defeat. I'll bet Esau noticed right away that something was different about his aggravating little brother. He noticed a new humility in him, a new tenderness. Let it be the same for each of us:

> May the God of hope fill you with all joy and peace as you trust in him, so that you may overflow with hope by the power of the Holy Spirit.
>
> Romans 15:13

GRIEF IS A FAMILY AFFAIR

Romans 12:15 tells us to "mourn with those who mourn."

Galatians 6:2 commands us to "carry each other's burdens, and in this way you will fulfill the law of Christ."

When I lost Hal, I was aware that I was not the only family member suffering through the grieving process. Hal's dear mother was suffering terribly over the loss of her son, and his daughters were grieving over the loss of their father. Hal's oldest grandchild (Mason) was grieving. So were his brother, his other family members, and the dozens of people who knew Hal as their friend.

In a Grief Group counseling session, I gained new insights into the circle of suffering. People of all ages and from all walks of life were there, looking for a way to get a handle on the grief that was consuming them. Tissue boxes lined the center of the table, within easy reach of those of us who needed them. And did we need them!

An elderly woman in a wheelchair described having just lost her husband after being his caregiver for fourteen years as he suffered with Parkinson's disease. Now, dealing with painful arthritis herself, she sits at home staring at the walls and wondering what's next in her life.

Two brothers who had recently lost their mother to cancer sat quietly in a corner. They had shared the burden of caring for their mom until the bitter end. Both of them were asking, "Why?" and, "What could we have done differently that might have kept our mother alive?"

A young wife told how her husband had gone away on a routine business trip a few days before Christmas. Then she got the call that he had died instantly of a heart attack. "I wasn't through with him yet!" she cried. "I wasn't even there. I don't know how much he suffered! I never got to say good-bye."

Another woman had helped her husband battle through three different cancers, each metastasizing to more serious places. She kept believing the doctors, that there was a chance he would live. Now she feels that she was a fool to believe them.

And then there was a man whose wife died in a car wreck two years ago. He wants to start dating, but his kids are unhappy about it. What should he do?

These are some of the faces from the secret society of sufferers. We just stumbled along, leaning on each other, weeping with each other, and gaining strength through our common pain. (See Widow's Appendix on page 229.)

As I drove home that day, I couldn't help but ask, "If you're going to lose a loved one, is it better that he or she should go fast—such as in a car crash or with a heart attack—or is it better to have them suffer for a while so good-byes can be said? I finally came to the conclusion that the loss of a loved one never seems fair, no matter how it happens. I'm sure that everyone in that room would have chosen another path.

I also thought a lot about what can be done to share the grief during a time of loss, and I decided that if you want to help someone who is grieving, the best thing is this:

Don't avoid that person. Be willing to be there, to just listen when they need to talk.

And help out if you can. Go over to the house, do the wash, clean up the kitchen. And by all means, act normally toward that person, the way you really are. If you're normally talkative, then be talkative. If you're usually quiet, it's okay to be quiet. Just be yourself!

But above all else, assure them that, "You did all you could do. You did a great job." Most folks tend to avoid those who are bereaved, thinking, "I just don't know what to say." But the grieving person needs to know that you are still their friend. I'm still pleased when someone calls to talk about pleasant memories of Hal. It hurts me when they won't even mention his name—as if he never existed.

DON'T SIGN UP FOR A GUILT TRIP

It's sad but true that victims often feel guilty. Those who have lost a spouse may think, "Why should I still be here when the person I loved so much has died?" Those who are left in the wake of a loved one's suicide have an especially difficult time of dealing with their pain and torment. "What could I have done differently?" "Why didn't I see it coming?" "How could he (she) do this to me?" These are only a few of the questions that plague those who have suffered terrible loss.

But you are not responsible for your loved one's death, whether from suicide, accident, disease, or any other reason. Every family member and close friend of someone who dies usually takes time to review their actions and often comes away feeling guilty for one reason or another.

The plain truth is that guilt shadows grief, just like lightning and thunder shadow a rainstorm. But you are not guilty! So forgive yourself, and move on.

Some people compound their feelings of guilt by feeling that tragedy came to them because God is punishing them. But here's what Dr. Paul Brand and Philip Yancey have to say in their wonderful book *The Gift of Pain:*

If God is using human suffering for punishment, he certainly has picked an obscure way to communicate his displeasure. The most basic fact about punishment is that it only works if the person knows the reason for it.[2]

Eastern religion has a fatalistic worldview: Things are the way they are meant to be. If God has chosen to bring disaster upon the people of Thailand, we should not interfere. Those who believe in karma believe that each person is in a state of cosmic flux, moving up and down the ladder of endless life cycles. Those who have been good will be better off in the next life; those who have not been good will be worse off.

But a Christian like Mother Teresa says we are compelled to respond to the needs we see and bring God's healing to those who are suffering.

In his book *Mandate for Mercy*, Don Stephens reports:

A group from YWAM (Youth With a Mission) was headed to minister to the Hmong in Thailand (Buddhists). Just before the group arrived, three newborn babies died of tetanus. The deaths were accepted fatalistically; obviously the babies were destined to die. No questions were asked. When the YWAM nurse arrived, she discovered the cause of the deaths had been the rusty knife the midwife had used to cut the cords. She instructed them on sterilizing the knives and many lives were saved.[3]

No, thank God, we don't get what we deserve—even if we imagine we deserve it. Christ paid the price for our sins when He died on the cross. Remember, He told us that it rains on the just and the unjust alike.

You Don't Have to Be a Victim

I must confess how easy it is for me to fall back into the "poor me" pit. Almost anything can trigger it: seeing a car like Hal's pass me on the road, hearing a song we liked, smelling his cologne in an elevator.

Whenever I am tempted to renew my membership in the "victim's club," I remember the advice given by Dr. Laura Schlesinger: "Misery is to be overcome, not used as a marinade."[4]

My assumption is that you also desire to reach for higher ground; that you are not choosing to stay "stuck" where you are. Perhaps you don't want to be a victim, but you're like the butterfly struggling to break out of its cocoon.

"Misery is to be overcome, not used as a marinade."

Remember that it is this very struggle that strengthens the butterfly's wings and makes her able to fly in the first place.

You and I have to resist the martyrdom that says, "I'm a victim; there is nothing I can do." With God's help, there is plenty we can do to overcome! As the old Quaker hymn says:

> Though He giveth or He taketh
> God His children ne'er forsaketh;
> His the loving purpose solely
> To preserve them, pure and holy.

Asking . . . and Acting!

Step 1: Asking

When God said no to His only Son's plea to take the terrible cup away, was it because He didn't care about His fears? Knowing that God said no to Jesus, how does that change your perspective on His negative responses to your pleadings?

Step 2: Acting

Is it possible to grieve in a hopeful way? Seems like the oxymoron of all oxymorons if you ask me. But I came up with a visual aid to help me. As I tried to put the pieces of my life back together, I knew there were some things I had to do, but that a lot of what needed to happen in my life was in the category of "Only God can do it." So I took a shoe box, cut a slit in the top, and wrote these bold letters on it:

S.F.J.T.D.
Something For Jesus To Do

I would write out my requests and prayers about things I knew I couldn't handle on my own, place them in the box, and then I'd try to stand back and let Jesus take care of them. After this, to remind myself that all of these cares and worries had been given over to God, on the side of the box I wrote:

Requests placed in this box will be addressed in God's time . . . not mine.
Be patient.
Once the concern is written and placed in this box, I will not hold on to it.
I will not try to figure out a solution.

I will surrender the problem to the Lord for a solution
. . . in His time.

Perhaps this seems a bit childish to you. But it certainly helped me and maybe will help you! Surrendering your worries to God can help you breathe easier through the hard times, and before you know it, that shoe box will be full of things you needed the Lord to handle. Past tense, because you'll find that He handled them, just like He did for me.

FOR BIBLE STUDY

Deuteronomy 30:19–20
Psalm 73:2–3
Luke 9:23
John 1:29; 14:18; 16:33; 20:25, 29
Romans 12:15; 15:13
Galatians 6:2
1 Thessalonians 4:13

TWELVE

WHEN IT RAINS IT POURS

---

*Water sustains us, but we can also drown in it. . . . Certain
genetic traits make us resistant to malaria, but the same genes
make us susceptible to other diseases. The risk of human
suffering simply is not avoidable in the world as we know it.*

John Sanders

Floods.

I know them well.

Perhaps, like me, you have found that the old saying is
true: When it rains, it pours.

In other words, you have been hit by a number of floods
and are digging yourself out from under the emotional
debris.

You're wondering if the good life has passed you by—
the life that's free of hassles, that's full of peace and ease.
But then again, if life were one never-ending process of
rolling "gently down the stream," I bet we'd all get bored
with it pretty quickly. For example, in California, where I
live, the weather is just about perfect every day of the year.

Often, I find myself longing for a change of seasons. Wouldn't it be great to see some beautiful fall colors? And how wonderful it would be to experience a white Christmas. How romantic!

But you know what? The folks who have to dig themselves out from under that white Christmas don't think it's so romantic. Human nature seems to be the same everywhere. We are never content with what we have, always thinking for some reason that the grass looks greener on the other side of the fence.

It's the same spiritually. We want only mountaintop experiences. Victories to celebrate. No valleys, thank you. No deserts. No dry spots. No cold spots. Nothing but warm fuzzies.

But when we signed up for the Christian faith, God didn't promise to put us in a little bubble and keep us safe and warm the rest of our lives. Anyone who teaches or believes this has set the stage to sabotage his faith.

WHY DO CHRISTIANS SUFFER?

After the dust was settling in my life, I began to think long and hard about why dedicated people of God may find themselves suffering. There are many reasons, including:

- Making mistakes or poor choices.
- Abusing our bodies by smoking, drinking too much, taking drugs, or not getting enough rest or exercise.
- Severing or damaging our connection with God.
- Needing to learn more about who God truly is.
- Being pruned to bear more fruit for God's kingdom.
- Having to learn compassion and godly character, and thus becoming more Christlike.
- Needing to learn what it is to "live by faith, not by sight" (2 Cor. 5:7)

166

Still, if you're like most folks I know, you're probably thinking, "All of this is well and good, but it doesn't account for what happened to me. That was just plain unfair!" I can relate to that.

But the Bible tells us that we are to endure hardship as soldiers of Christ. God's will for us is not always the easy path, the way of least resistance.

Satan doesn't work for God; he's self-employed.

I believe it's human nature to resist hardship. We rebuke the devil for anything that infringes on our comfort zone. We look for the quick fix and the easy way out. But when we do this, we are copying the ways of the world, which advises those who are troubled to "take a little drink," or "snort some cocaine," or pop a prescription "happy pill" as a way of covering up pain and sorrow. But taking the easy way out is not the answer to suffering. It only leads to more suffering.

Facing an unwanted pregnancy? Abortion is not the answer. It will lead to additional problems in your life.

Trapped in a difficult marriage? A divorce may seem to be the solution, but in the end it will lead to so many more complications.

The world's answers always appear to be easy at the beginning—but so hard at the end. God's answers are usually tough at the beginning, but so peaceable at the end.

I had to reconcile myself to the idea that in the troubles I was facing, God might be working out His plan. Let's get rid of the idea that God uses Satan to beat us up and do His dirty work. Remember, Satan doesn't work for God; he's self-employed.

Sometimes we make the mistake of thinking that Satan is God's opposite number. But he's not. Satan isn't all-powerful; he is not present everywhere at the same time; he is not the anti-god. He is an angel, a created being who could be crushed beneath God's feet in an instant if God chose to crush him. I love what C. S. Lewis wrote about Satan: "It is so stupid of modern civilization to have given up believing in the devil when he is the only explanation of it!"[1]

As a sci-fi fan, I love Lewis's "space trilogy" novels, in which he talks about the planet earth being described by other creatures throughout the universe as "the Dark Planet." I wonder if Lewis may have been onto something very important.

Out of all the choices in the solar system, God chose to banish the fallen angel, Lucifer, to the earth. Jesus testified, "I saw Satan fall like lightning from heaven." And he took with him one-third of the angels to reign in this new territory.

That explains so much about the unfairness and injustices of life. Couple the reality of Satan's power with man's fallen nature, and you've set up a scenario for some terrible things to happen to some most undeserving people. Ah, the warm fuzzies we get from the melodious old hymn "This Is My Father's World." But that's not the whole story. True, this world is God's good creation. But not everything that happens on this "dark planet" is necessarily God's will. In fact, Jesus tells us we must pray that God's will would be done on earth as it is in heaven.

Again and again, the Bible emphasizes that this is *not* our Father's world in the way God created it to be—the way it was before sin entered the picture and messed things up, like a vandal splashing paint on a beautiful Rembrandt.

- In John 17:15, Jesus says of His disciples, "My prayer is not that you take them out of the world but that you protect them from the evil one."

- In John 14:30, as the time for His betrayal and cruci-fixion drew near, Jesus said, "I will not speak with you much longer, for the prince of this world is coming."
- The apostle John echoed this thought in 1 John 5:19: "We know that we are children of God, and that the whole world is under the control of the evil one."
- And in 2 Corinthians 4:4, the apostle Paul wrote, "The god of this age has blinded the minds of unbe-lievers, so that they cannot see the light of the gospel of the glory of Christ, who is the image of God." The King James Version uses "world" in place of "age."

These verses and many others speak of the influence Satan has on this planet of ours. But we can rest assured that Independence Day is coming!

SUFFERING AND EVIL ARE NOT SYNONYMOUS

When all the unfairness of life—every injustice you could imagine—began to fall on the Son of God, He never cried, "Unfair!" He was in the habit of factoring His Father into every situation that came His way. Yes, He was human enough to cry, "If it is possible, may this cup be taken from me," but He also added, "Yet not as I will, but as you will" (Matt. 26:39).

We are wrong if we think that suffering and evil are the same thing. They're not. Otherwise, the Beatitudes make no sense. How could Jesus say that those who mourn are "blessed" if mourning is evil? How could He pronounce a blessing upon those who are being persecuted if persecu-tion is something that God's people will never experience? You see, He was looking at things from another perspec-tive, knowing the end from the beginning. He knew that suffering was going to produce its perfect fruit in time, and that those who patiently endured for God's sake would one day be rewarded with unspeakable joy.

169

As singer-songwriter Jamie Owens Collins expresses it in her song "Seasons of the Soul":

> A season in the rain will end at last,
> A season full of pain will surely pass,
> The reason will be plain someday
> When love reveals its goal.
> Such are the seasons of the soul.[2]

For us to have a planet where we all got everything we liked and none of us ever had any problems—eternal spring—God would have to control us like robots. Only then would there be no disease, divorce, drunk drivers, sex-

In order to have this utopia we desire, God would have to do a free-will recall.

ual abuse, crime, or poverty. The court system would be fair, relationships would be simple and honest, and life would go on without a hitch.

The only catch would be that no one would freely love God. We'd all be programmed "Stepford Wives" or "Robocops." We'd obey automatically, and that would be so unsatisfying to the Creator!

THE FALL GUY

If I had accepted the fact that pain and suffering are going to be a part of our human experience, I would have been less vulnerable. But instead, when something goes wrong, it is my human nature to immediately roll my eyes toward heaven and say sarcastically: "Hey, God, thanks a lot. I really needed this!" But how and when did God suddenly become the scapegoat for everything that goes wrong on this planet?

I have an understanding of this concept because I've been through some earthquakes! I have cracks on my patio and in the foundation of my home. But when I checked with my homeowners' insurance for a repair estimate they said, "Sorry. We're not responsible for 'acts of God.'" Hmmmm?

I thought of Elijah, who heard God in a still small voice but couldn't find Him anywhere in a natural disaster:

> Then a great and powerful wind tore the mountains apart and shattered the rocks before the LORD, but the LORD was not in the wind. After the wind there was an earthquake, but the LORD was not in the earthquake. After the earthquake came a fire, but the LORD was not in the fire.
>
> 1 Kings 19:11–12

So it's not true! God doesn't sit in heaven feeling ticked off at the strange people who live in California and say, "I think I'll send them a little 6.5 on the Richter scale. Let's see how they like those apples!" No, the Bible tells us that

Natural disasters are not an act of Father God; they're an act of Mother Nature

God is not the one who sends earthquakes and hurricanes upon the world. He is the One who grieves with us when we encounter such sorrows.

In the thirteenth chapter of Luke, Jesus talks about eighteen people who were killed when a tower fell on them. He says, "Do you think they were more guilty than all the others living in Jerusalem? I tell you, no!" (v. 4). In essence, He was saying, "Get real, people. These things happen, and God is not to blame. Sometimes the best people get caught in the middle of something terrible. Sometimes the worst people escape unharmed."

You and I are not just pawns in some celestial chess game.

Theologian John Sanders, who was quoted at the beginning of this chapter, writes:

> If it is believed that God created a world in which air currents and water vapor bring needed rain, and God cannot prevent these elements from sometimes forming hurricanes, then God takes the risk that people will suffer from them and may turn away from his love.[3]

WHAT ABOUT PREDESTINATION?

I've already told you that I was raped when I was a teenager, became pregnant as a result, and gave birth to a beautiful baby girl. (The story is told in my book, *The Missing Piece*.)

Not long ago, I was being interviewed on a secular radio program, as my daughter (the lovely result of that rape) sat beside me.

When I finished my story, the interviewer said, "Oh, what a beautiful God-story, then. So it was God who sent that man out to rape you so you could have this baby?"

I swallowed hard and spat out the words, "No! Because I don't believe the God of the Bible causes evil. But I believe He is the only One Who can make *good* out of the *evil*."

"Good answer, gal," the interviewer caustically replied.

He was hitting upon an interesting question that has nagged Christians for centuries. Causation is the sticky business: Who instigated what? How much does God predestine to happen, and how much does He merely allow? There's no getting away from the fact that the crucifixion was planned by God many thousands of years before it actually took place.

It was preordained that Judas Iscariot would play a major part in that plan by betraying Christ to the authorities. Here's how Peter put it in his sermon on Pentecost: "This man was handed over to you by God's set purpose and foreknowledge; and you, with the help of wicked men, put him to death by nailing him to the cross" (Acts 2:23).

So was Judas a helpless pawn in God's scheme? No, he was "a wicked man," and God used Judas's wickedness to help bring about the salvation of humankind.

God seems to permit all sorts of things He doesn't solicit or desire, and if those situations are given over to Him, He can find a way to bring good out of them. But God does not nod approvingly when another earthquake smashes through California. He doesn't smile when He sees drug pushers hanging around junior high schools. He did not fire up the anti-Semitic anger of Adolf Hitler.

Yes, the Bible says, "The lot is cast into the lap, but its every decision is from the LORD" (Prov. 16:33). But that does not mean that God is the one who picks the winner in a horse race or the Power Ball lottery.

Proverbs also says, in the first verse of chapter 21, that, "The king's heart is in the hand of the LORD; he directs it like a watercourse wherever he pleases." But this obviously does not mean that every decision a national leader makes is directed by God. Otherwise, there would be no cruel dictators in the world who made decisions based on their own greed rather than on what was good for the people they govern. Unfortunately, we know the world is full of such ruthless dictators!

But it seems natural to desperately grasp for someone to blame. Even the disciples didn't grasp this concept. When a blind man approached Jesus, they asked the Master: "Rabbi, who sinned, this man or his parents, that he was born blind?" (John 9:2). Jesus' heart must have sunk; they *still* weren't getting this. He replied, "Neither this man nor his parents sinned

173

. . . but this happened so that the work of God might be displayed in his life" (v. 3). And Jesus healed his blindness.

That blind man, much like us, did nothing to deserve his plight. No one sinned to cause it. No one was to blame. We don't get what we deserve anyhow (thank God). The wise psalmist reminds us: "He does not treat us as our sins deserve or repay us according to our iniquities" (Ps. 103:10). Is God punishing you with this affliction? No! The fact that something bad has happened to you does not indicate you are somehow paying for your sins. But God would hope to use this experience, like the blind man's disability, to display His awesome power. Right now, Jesus may be waiting for you to come to Him. No judgment, no questions asked. He doesn't want us to waste our sorrows but to place them in His hand. Hand over your unanswered questions. Don't remain in a hurting state when God desires to work it all together for your ultimate good.

Another verse that causes some people trouble is Lamentations 3:37: "Who can speak and have it happen if the Lord has not decreed it?"

This doesn't mean that every angry mother who tells her son "You're grounded" is speaking something the Lord has decreed. Nor does it mean that any nervous single who asks for a date (or the nervous person who accepts or refuses that date) is acting out the Lord's decree! Such things are not predestined by the Almighty. God has no robot army on earth. But we can also conclude that, if the Bible is right, nothing happens on this planet that is outside of His knowledge or "permissive" will.

GOD USES ORDINARY PEOPLE

When I was in the darkest days of my own experience, still grieving over the loss of my husband, still reeling from the news that I also had cancer, I experienced no visitation from an angel of light. There were many times when I tried to get some inspiration from the Scriptures, and they were as dry as the stock market page in the daily newspaper.

But then the phone would ring, or a friend would show up at my door. They were the hands and feet of Jesus. They brought His love and comfort to me, thereby fulfilling the words of Christ, who said, "I was sick and you looked after me, I was in prison and you came to visit me." And "Whatever you did for one of the least of these brothers of mine, you did for me" (Matt. 25:36, 40).

These ordinary people were extraordinary examples of the love of God and proof of the Bible's teaching that "a friend loves at all times."

TEMPTED IN THE DESERT

In my desert places—when I was feeling most deserted—I discovered how many friends really cared for me.

When some friends disappeared, I discovered that God alone is sufficient. There is always something to be gained, something to be learned, and the driest place in the desert may be where God plans to show you His power and the provision He has made for your life. It is during the driest times—when we are tempted to forsake our faith—that we have to dig deeper to find God's life-giving water.

Jesus was tempted in the wilderness for forty days and forty nights, during which Satan showed Jesus all the kingdoms of the world and said, "I will give you all their authority and splendor, for it has been given to me, and I can give it to anyone I want to. So if you worship me, it will all be yours" (Luke 4:6–7). (I find it interesting that Jesus didn't contradict Satan's claims to possession of this world's kingdoms.)

If Jesus had any idea of the suffering that lay before Him—and surely He did—then why did He refuse the devil's offer? Again, Jesus refused to take the easy way out. He was committed to fulfilling the Father's plan of redemption, even though He knew it would lead to His own humiliation and suffering.

SPENDING THE NIGHT WITH JOB

As I've gone through my time in the wilderness, I have spent many nights sitting up with a biblical character named Job. Bible scholars tell us that Job is probably the oldest book in the Bible, and it's also one of the hardest to figure out. I was thinking of Job when a friend asked me, "Would a grief counselor help you?" And I said, "I don't need a counselor. I need a theologian to get things sorted out!"

Although God permitted Job's trials He did not actually instigate them.

When I first started reading this book, it really bugged me. I mean, here was a righteous dude, a guy who was "blameless and upright, a man who fears God and shuns evil" (Job 1:8). And yet he went through absolute hell on earth! At first glance, it seems that Job became a simple pawn in a game of chess between God and the devil. But the questions raised in the Book of Job have as much to do with free will as they do with suffering. Would Job *choose* to turn to God, or would he *choose* to turn away?

In the first part of this book, God asks the devil what he's been doing with himself these days, and the devil replies that he has been "roaming through the earth and going back and forth in it" (Job 1:7). I sense a bit of territorial bragging here, don't you? It also reminds me of the Bible's caution that "Your enemy the devil prowls around like a roaring lion looking for someone to devour" (1 Peter 5:8).

When God calls Satan's attention to Job, the devil dismisses the man's faithfulness. He says in essence, "No wonder he's such a goody-goody. Look at all the stuff you've given him." Satan says, "Have you not put a hedge around him and his household and everything he has?" (Job 1:10).

And it was true. God *had* built a protective hedge around Job, as He does for His people. We are to trust Him to keep that hedge of protection firm. In God's plan for my life the hedge was lowered enough to allow some challenging problems to attack me, but not low enough to allow the angel of death to claim my life. (Although I've gotta tell you, if he looked like that handsome angel of death on TV's *Touched by an Angel*, I might have been tempted.)

Anyway, God knows full well that Job's faithfulness has nothing to do with his prosperity and offers to lower the "hedge" around Job so Satan can give him a quick punch or two.

Well, over the next few weeks, Job's life became a mess. You've heard of a rags to riches story. Job went from riches to rags and then some!

But who put Job through all these trials? There's no getting around the fact that they were approved to be included in God's plan for Job's life. And God offers no explanation, other than what is revealed in the Scriptures we've already noted.

Satan filled out his requisition, but God had to give authorization before he could attack Job. Even Job recognized that this was true, and perhaps that's what helped him get through it all with his sanity intact. In the end, Job overcame Satan by the Word of God and the power of his testimony. It's important to keep in mind that although God permitted Job's trials He did not actually instigate them.

You see, the Book of Job shows us that God may allow many things He doesn't particularly approve of. Job must have realized this, as it is recorded, "Job did not sin by charging God with wrongdoing" (Job 1:22). God didn't load millions of His innocent Jewish people on trains headed for death camps during World War II. Nor does He single-handedly strategize against any one of us as individuals. He tolerates cancer and puts up with watching people unjustly treated in hospitals. But it is people who do the wrong things, not God.

Some ask, "But if He has the power to intervene, then why doesn't He?" Perhaps He is just permitting sin to run its natural course so it can be exposed for what it truly is. There could be no greater proof of the fact that when people are not connected with God through Christ, they can be a depraved menace to themselves and everyone else they meet. After all, it is people, not God, who have mass-produced weapons of destruction, who have polluted our air and water, and who have perpetuated greed, stress, and injustice in the legal system.

In his classic book *The Problem of Pain*, C. S. Lewis writes, "When souls become wicked they will certainly use this possibility to hurt one another, and this, perhaps, accounts for four-fifths of the sufferings of men."[4]

God doesn't cause suffering. We are the ones who cause suffering by refusing to take proper care of ourselves, by trying to cover up our pain with alcohol and drugs, by hardening our hearts so that we are no longer moved when we see people in desperate need.

A friend of mine relates that when she first saw the homeless people who inhabit downtown Los Angeles, she prayed, "Lord, why don't You do something about this?" Within her heart, she heard His answer: "I have done something. I've shown it to you."

WHERE'S THE DIVINE INTERVENTION?

A friend of mine who was a victim of incest once asked me, "Where was God for me? Can you answer that?"

As my heart filled with compassion for her, I sputtered, "I'm guessing He was at the same place He was when He watched them nail His only Son to the cross."

What is God doing when crummy things happen to us? I believe He's weeping with us. And at the same time, I believe He's shaping a plan to incorporate that hurtful experience into something good, into something that will help us fulfill the potential He has placed within us, to become everything He has always intended us to be.

If He chose to, God could come down, be interviewed on CNN, and explain why He sometimes seems to be indifferent to our suffering. But He chose not to do that. Instead, He supplied the only answer we need when He sent His own Son down to experience pain and suffering for Himself. Since the time when Jesus walked on this planet, no one could ever accuse God of not understanding what we go through.

I also believe that God does intervene in many ways we do not see. I still believe He is in control in a most underground and discreet way. Think about what life on earth would be like if Satan had free rein to do anything he chose. This planet would be unlivable. People would be buying tickets for orgies involving human sacrifice. Crimes like murder, rape, and child molestation would be overlooked by society. Should I go on? Thank God, Satan does not set the world's agenda, but it is restricted by the Creator.

WITH FRIENDS LIKE THESE, WHO NEEDS ENEMIES?

One of the things that really gets to me when I read the story of Job is the arrogance and self-righteousness of his friends. You can die from such friends as Job had! And as sorry as I am to say it, the descendants of those friends are alive and well in the church today. I know because I've met many of them. They told me that I must have done something to cause God to bring suffering into my life, and that I needed to examine myself so I could figure out what it was! Yes, there are still plenty of Pharisees telling suffering people that they must have done something to deserve it.

Here are just a few of what such "Job's comforters" have said to me:

- Maybe God is trying to teach you something.
- You should feel privileged that God thinks you're this strong.
- Just concentrate on your blessings—you still have your own life.
- What a wonderful chance to grow in faith! God has promised He won't give you more than you're able to take, so apparently this is within the legal limit.
- Don't complain or feel sorry for yourself, or you may lose your blessing.

This kind of advice is nothing more than what I call V.R.G.—verbalized religious garbage. If someone confronts you with such a judgmental spirit, I urge you to shake the dust off your feet and move on! One of baseball's great pitchers, Dave Dravecky, who lost his pitching arm to cancer, wrote about the guilt people can unintentionally put on you when you are suffering:

> False guilt is a burden that keeps hurting people from discovering the peace, hope and encouragement that is necessary to endure suffering.[5]

When God finally revealed Himself to Job, He still didn't explain why Job had to suffer. In fact, God asked all the questions, instead of the other way around. But as Max Lucado says:

> God's questions aren't intended to teach; they are intended to stun. They aren't intended to enlighten; they are intended to awaken. They aren't intended to stir the mind; they are intended to bend the knees.[6]

Frankly, I'm encouraged by the fact that even though Job was a good and righteous man, he was still confused and troubled by what he went through. He got so low he even cursed the day he was born and said he wished he had died at birth. Even so, God never scolded him for his doubts, fears, and discouragement. This book sends a strong message that there is nothing we can say to the Almighty that will take Him by surprise. As I said in the last chapter, it is important to be honest with God, even if it means expressing anger and disappointment to Him.

Experiences have the power to make us bitter or better.

It comforts me to know that you and I are in very good company when we suffer for no apparent reason. Job was not the first, nor the last, good person who suffered unjustly. Job illustrates for us what power we have—to choose to serve God despite the afflictions we might be passing through. Job's story also shows us that there is an omnipotent God who is willing to share His powerful presence with us while we go through our trials. Yes, we must accept it all—the good, the bad, and the ugly, the sunshine and the rain. Job summed it up when he said, "Shall we accept good from God, and not trouble?" (Job 2:10).

It's Not Over 'til It's Over

Why are you suffering? I can't tell you. But I can promise you that you will understand in God's time. He may show you the purpose of it all now, or you may have to wait. The old hymn says that we'll understand it all "by and by."

181

But until we come face-to-face with the King of Truth, we'll have to trust Him with the other half of the story.

Right now, Jesus is waiting for you to come to Him. He doesn't want you to waste your sorrows, but rather to place them in His hands.

So if you haven't done so, hand over all your unanswered questions to Him now. Don't remain in a hurting state when you can "know that in all things God works for the good of those who love him" (Rom. 8:28). Come to Jesus now and begin to experience "the peace of God, which transcends all understanding" (Phil. 4:7).

🌿Asking . . . and Acting!

Step 1: Asking

If you plant a seed and see no apparent growth for two weeks, is the seed dormant? If you cry out to God to heal your suffering and it endures, is it because He is not working?

Step 2: Acting

Are you suffering and questioning and getting no answers? It may be helpful to do a little biblical "word study." Take your Bible and a good concordance to a quiet place and spend some time looking up all of the references to the word *suffering*. You may want to make a list of the things you learn.

After you have read through all the Scripture references, pray that God will give you ears to hear whatever He wants you to learn from your word study. Think about the verses you read and review your notes to see if there is a personal message that jumps out at you.

For Bible Study

1 Kings 19:11–12
Job 1:7–8, 10, 22
Psalms 103:10
Proverbs 16:33; 21:1
Lamentations 3:37
Matthew 25:36, 40; 26:39
Luke 4:6–7, 13:4

John 9:2–3; 14:30; 17:15
Acts 2:23
Romans 8:28
2 Corinthians 4:4
Philippians 4:7
1 Peter 5:8
1 John 5:19

THIRTEEN

FRUIT FROM THE TREE OF LIFE

---

*He is like a tree planted by streams of water,
which yields its fruit in season.*

Psalm 1:3

Knowledge.

Education and enlightenment. I was sure these were all I needed to answer my nagging questions about life's struggles. If I could just study more and uncover the hidden secrets, I'd be wiser and more at peace. But apparently God doesn't put the premium on scholarship that we do.

Do you realize that the Omniscient God of the universe has no college degree? Perhaps these are some of the reasons:

- He had only one major publication.
- This publication was in Hebrew and had no references.
- Some even doubted He authored the publication.
- It may be true that He created the world, but what has He done since then?

- He rarely came to class. He just told his students to "read the Book."
- His office hours were infrequent and were usually held on a mountaintop.
- He sent His Son to teach the class.

In my quest for knowledge I came across the two trees in the Garden of Eden: the Tree of the Knowledge of Good and Evil and the Tree of Life. God gave Adam strict instructions to avoid the Tree of the Knowledge of Good and Evil. This was the only tree he and Eve were not to eat from because it would bring death.

You see, Adam and Eve were never created to die. Our bodies and spirits were created for life. (Perhaps this is why the death realm is so hard for us to comprehend—we were not wired to understand it.) But the mystery of the Tree of the Knowledge of Good and Evil was intriguing. The idea of knowledge was—and is—tempting. We want answers to every question imaginable. We want answers to the mystery of death and suffering.

What if God is more interested in satisfying our hearts than our heads? Maybe He would rather we come to Him as children with outstretched arms instead of as knowledge-seekers with notebooks in hand. Proverbs 3:5 warns, "Lean not on your own understanding," yet we continually rely on knowing, on comprehending, on getting a grip on the answers.

BARKING UP THE WRONG TREE

I was on a quest. I tenaciously held on to the idea that I would have peace if I could satisfy my head with the reasons why my world had crumbled. So I made an appointment with an old, wise professor of theology. I explained that I needed his input, as I was writing a book on the purpose of pain. I came prepared with a yellow pad filled with questions.

Peering at me over the rim of his half-glasses, he took my yellow pad and flipped through the pages.

"Why are you so intent on having the answers to these questions?" he asked.

Rather than seeking the purpose, seek the presence of the Prince of Peace.

That was easy. "I want to pass them on to others who suffer."

He smiled all too knowingly. "Instead of encouraging your readers to seek the *purpose* of God, encourage them to seek the *presence* of God. Then all these things will be added to them."

How did he do that? I thought in amazement. In only a couple of sentences, he had answered it all.

We have a choice as to what we will seek: forbidden knowledge or the life that comes from God. I've finally turned away from my insatiable need for answers to unanswerable questions. I've made a choice to refuse to dance around the tree that promises those answers. I'd rather eat from the Tree of Life, cultivating God's life and nature within me.

As I surrender my questions, I'm experiencing the satisfying presence of God. Since I've given up on seeking to know the purpose for the suffering and losses in my life (and the lives of my friends), I'm finding that peace that passes understanding.

The cunning serpent enticed Eve to eat from the wrong tree. (And note gals: Eve got her directions about the tree not from God but from Adam. Could her mate have possibly mumbled something to her without communicating clearly? Such things have been known to happen.) The forbidden fruit began to sound alluring. Besides, it was "pleasing to the eye, and also desirable for gaining wisdom" (Gen. 3:6). What a deal! Eat some fruit and become wise. Satan seduced her, saying, "Your eyes will be opened and you will be like God" (v. 4).

The power of His presence is more satisfying than the power of knowing all the answers.

Despite what we may think, that's exactly what we *don't* want. Is it our goal to become our own gurus? We would then be so self-sufficient and independent, with all the answers in our back pockets, that we wouldn't need to depend on the Lord.

My friend and fellow speaker Peggy Benson helped her husband, Bob, battle cancer for fourteen years. In his last days, she asked him if the Lord had ever told him the "why" of this suffering. Bob replied, "Yes, and He said to me, 'Bob, why do you keep asking Me that question? When I get you to the place where you'll know the answer, the question won't matter anymore.'"

The Spirit of God is the Comforter. He wants to come to us, not to satisfy all our questions, but to surround and fill us with the presence of God and make those answers unimportant. He cares enough to give us the power to choose to walk with Him, even when life is not fair.

HEAVENLY COMMUNICATIONS

For months after my husband died I had an intense longing to talk to him. I would have been willing to do almost anything to have just five more minutes with him.

But the Bible forbids us to attempt to contact the dead. (Yes, Jesus was on earth for a few days after His resurrection, but He retained His bodily form—nail scars and all. He was no ghost.)

I have heard that some people seem to sense a lingering presence in the first days after a loved one is gone. I never felt that with my husband, as I know there is a "great gulf fixed" (Luke 16:26) between heaven and earth and it is not to be explored. I will admit, however, that I can't resist saying hello to Hal whenever I see a picture of him, hear a song we loved, etc. I realize I'm simply releasing more grief. I don't expect him to hear or respond.

Still, one day when I was thinking about how much I'd like to talk to him, or perhaps get a message to him, I remembered Hebrews 1:14 (KJV). The angels are described as "ministering spirits, sent forth to minister for them who shall be heirs of salvation."

I choose to live the life I didn't choose,
and I plan to live the life I didn't plan.

Hmmm, I thought. If the angels of God are messengers, maybe I could ask one of them to get a message to Hal! (Now I realize some readers will be tempted to think I'm an oddball, but only another bereaved person can understand my desperation.)

So one Tuesday I prayed, "Lord, if it's okay with You, I'd like to request that an angel take a message to Hal just this once. Tell him three things—that I love him, that God is helping me, and that I'm still using his handicapped parking card." Hal had been issued a temporary handicapped parking sticker, which we would hang on the rearview mirror. Someone—okay, I admit it, it was me—tampered with it a bit and punched a new hole in it to extend its expiration date.

I just wanted to use it until my treatments were completed. Did I know this was illegal? Yes, I confess I did. But it was so convenient, and I told myself that I had a legitimate reason to use the card—with my apologies to the disabled community.

Back to my story. I thought it was the perfect message to send to Hal. He would certainly know for sure that it was from crazy Lee, and he would laugh saying, "Go for it! That's my girl."

The next morning, Wednesday, I felt elated as I finished my last radiation treatment and was given a Certificate of Congratulations from the Cancer Center. I went to the market and parked in a handicapped parking spot. When I came out, there were two police cars blocking my van. Four officers were waiting for me. I swallowed hard.

"Is this your vehicle, ma'am?"

"Yes, sir."

"I need your license, registration, and that handicapped card."

They took the documents back to their squad cars to use the computer for verification. Needless to say, I was sweating bullets. The young officer returned.

"This card has expired and is registered only to Harold Ezell. Are you driving him around today?"

I fought back the tears. "Oh, I wish I were. But no, he died from cancer."

There was a pause before he continued. "Do you know who tampered with this handicapped card? Do you realize this is a felony offense?"

I confessed. "I changed it. I wanted to extend it. After Hal died I found out that I too had cancer. I completed my last treatment this morning. This was a happy day for me." I showed him my Certificate of Congratulations.

He stared at me for a moment and walked back to the other officers. As they talked, I pictured myself being handcuffed in the parking lot and hauled off to jail. This was not something I wanted to add to my testimony!

Then the officer returned and handed me all of the documents. "Mrs. Ezell," he began, "I could have you taken in, fine you for tampering with the card, and also fine you for parking illegally in a handicapped zone. But in light of what you've been through, we're going to let you go with a simple parking ticket. I'll be keeping the handicapped card."

I took the ticket and thanked him for his kindness. The police cars drove off, and I drove slowly to a deserted part of the parking lot, my hands shaking on the wheel. What did this mean? I'd been using the card for months, but just eighteen hours after I had asked an angel to deliver my message to Hal it was gone. Was there a connection?

I must admit I never received any big revelation. I began to reason that if God had permitted my message to get through to Hal in heaven, then he would be a different Hal than the joker I had known here on earth. In the purity and righteousness of heaven, Hal would not have laughed (as I initially supposed he might). Hal may very well have replied to that angel, "Well, you get that card away from her. That's illegal."

Maybe my request never got past God, Who also wouldn't have thought my little joke was funny. Maybe the Lord was the one to say, "Lee, this is not funny. You can't rightly use a handicapped spot. I'll take that card away from you tomorrow."

And bingo! Less than twenty-four hours after I prayed, I was cardless. Maybe I was truly touched by an angel.

The Mystery of Suffering and Death

In the movie *Rudy*, the title character was diligent in pursuing his dream of playing football for the University of Notre Dame. When he questioned why God had not allowed his dream to be fulfilled, a wise priest simply replied, "I know two things in life: There is a God, and I am not Him."

We have so many questions about suffering and death. It seems Christianity is the only religion that doesn't claim to have all the answers. Indeed, all the cults and false religions have their "ducks in a row" when it comes to trying to satisfy our curiosity.

In Islam the answer is "It is the will of Allah," which no one is allowed to question. To the Hindus it's all about recycling: Suffering in this life will improve your karma for your next life. (They'll even take it a little further: If a baby dies, there was bad karma in the baby's soul!) To the Buddhists it's about the circle of life, which Satan holds in his power. (If we could end suffering, we would reach Nirvana.) In many religions, life is all about fatalism: *que sera sera*, whatever will be will be. We are powerless to effect change. Answers like predestination and reincarnation seem to fit. Their gods supply all the answers. All you have to do is read the pamphlet.

We don't have all the answers, but we know who does!

But Christianity *is not* a system of tips and techniques supplied for our satisfaction. The one true God cannot be tamed and placed in a cage to be analyzed by His creation. We cannot perform tests on Him and publish the results. Yet in one way, God did put Himself on public display for all to see and hear so we can draw our own conclusions about Him. When God was born as a man on earth (Jesus), everyone could hear

Him, talk with Him, and witness His character firsthand. The Word was made flesh and lived among us.

We need to grasp the fact that God is not obligated to explain His actions to us. Whenever I'm confused about how God has dealt with someone, I go to Deuteronomy

Christianity is not a system of tips and techniques supplied for our satisfaction.

29:29: "The secret things belong to the LORD our God." Isaiah said, "Truly you are a God who hides himself" (45:15). Maybe that's what Jesus was echoing when He said, "I praise you, Father, Lord of heaven and earth, because you have hidden these things from the wise and learned, and revealed them to little children" (Matt. 11:25).

We are choosing to be childlike in turning away from the tantalizing Tree of Knowledge when we realize that seeking after all the answers is not satisfying. It is only frustrating. I expect that what I understand now is like seeing through a glass darkly.

We don't like to see things darkly. We want them to make sense to us. When they don't, confusion can set in and faith can begin to unravel. Christ's disciples, as well as many political and war heroes, died with dignity and confidence, because they understood why they were suffering and believed that their suffering was inevitable.

I know only in part, as this poem expresses:

I asked for strength and God gave me difficulties to
    make me strong.
I asked for wisdom and God gave me problems to solve.

I asked for prosperity and God gave me brawn and brain
    to work.
I asked for courage and God gave me dangers to overcome.
I asked for patience and God placed me in situations
    where I was forced to wait.
I asked for love and God gave me troubled people to
    help.
I asked for favors and God gave me opportunities.
I received nothing I wanted.
I received everything I needed.
And my prayer has been answered!

                                        Anonymous

SEEKING GOD'S HEART, NOT HIS HAND

In Bible school we burned the midnight oil. It took hours
to memorize the books of the Bible, the prophets, chronol-
ogy, and Scripture verses. I remember the night the Lord
caught me up short.

"You diligently study the Scriptures because you think
that by them you possess eternal life. These are the Scriptures that testify about me, yet you refuse to come to me to
have life" (John 5:39).

Whoa! Wait a minute, I thought. I don't want to be an
expert on the Book. I want to know the Author.

Seeking the face of the Lord is different from seeking a
handout. This is my highest desire and the place where I've
found the most comfort—in seeking His face. Second
Chronicles 7:14 tells us the great things that will happen
when we humble ourselves, pray, and seek God's face. But
so often we would rather have the divine handout. We cry,
"Come on, God, fork it over! Let us know the answers.
Give us the information we seek."

Deuteronomy 29:29 says, "The secret things belong to
the LORD our God, but the things revealed belong to us
and to our children forever."

Many things are kept secret from us. Why? I guess they are on a need-to-know basis, and we don't need to know. Yet we seem to think that if we could grasp the reason why we'd be better off.

But how could we grasp the reason why a child is born with severe learning disabilities? Why a drunk driver broadsided the car that night? Why, after years of marriage, a

I don't want to know the Rule Book better than I know the Ruler.

man would suddenly walk away from it all, leaving his wife and children devastated.

Do we have the capacity to comprehend the reason for such things? A nuclear physicist can attempt to explain a complicated theory to a seven-year-old, but try as he might, the child would be unable to grasp it. In the same way, I think that many of the unexplained secrets of suffering are beyond us. And even if we were to understand the depth of the meaning, it still wouldn't satisfy the pain we feel.

There have been some things revealed to us through the experience—and we can learn something if we are willing. I've seen the condition of my heart, the anger and sense of being stranded. I've wrestled with the unfairness of life, and I've been down for the count.

Yet I can honestly say to you that underneath it all, I've sensed the everlasting arms. I've leaned on them for survival. I've found God faithful and consistent, with the grace I needed, at the crisis moment when I needed it (although I wanted it before then!). I've experienced the warmth and comfort of the Scriptures to my cold soul. And I have never before experienced the closeness of God's Spirit as I did when I cried out in agony.

Let's face it. If we had all the answers neatly boxed up for us, we wouldn't need faith. We wouldn't really need that type of God either. He would be too predictable. We'd have Him all figured out. We would be left with a neat little formula where we could simply plug in the variables and come up with all the answers.

When we finally wake up and realize our questions really don't need specific answers, we can begin enjoying the warmth of His presence in all life's circumstances.

The New Testament records what happened when some very frightened disciples were caught in a violent storm out on the Sea of Galilee. They were afraid their boat was about

Peace is not the absence of conflict,
but the presence of God
in the middle of conflict.

to sink and may have felt the way you feel right now. Yes, Jesus was in their boat, but He was sleeping. (Sleeping? In a small boat during a squall? It doesn't seem possible. I wonder if the Teacher may have been waiting to see how they would handle this crisis.) When His disciples shook Him awake, He rebuked the storm and the winds quieted immediately.

But then Jesus turned to them, asking, "Why are you so afraid? Do you still have no faith?" (Mark 4:40).

The Master may seem to be sleeping right now as far as you're concerned. At least, He doesn't appear to be involved and working on your problem. But if you've invited Jesus into your life, that means He's in your boat. And that, in turn, means you have no reason to fear and can begin to rely on your faith to bring stability to your life.

If we concentrate on seeking God's face now and not on stretching ourselves to see into the future, we will hear the Lord speaking to us. As Elisabeth Elliot so eloquently phrased it:

> Today is mine. Tomorrow is none of my business. If I peer anxiously into the fog of the future, I will strain my spiritual eyes so that I will not see clearly what is required of me **now**.[1]

Finally, my prayers began to change. "I'm so hungry, Lord, my spiritual stomach is growling. I need a good portion of the bread that comes from heaven. *You* are that bread, the Bread of Life. If I eat of You while in this desert place, I will not starve to death. Though I desire the meat of understanding, I put that desire aside. O Bread of Life, I will be satisfied with the manna You send me in my wilderness!"

I love the way Annie Chapman puts it in her beautiful poem *The Tapestry*:

> My life is but a weaving between my Lord and me;
> I cannot choose the colors He worketh steadily.
> Oft'times He weaveth sorrow, and I in foolish pride
> Forget that He seeth the upper, and I the underside.
> Not 'til the loom is silent, and the shutters cease to fly,
> Shall God unroll the canvas and explain the reason why
> The dark threads are as needful in the Weaver's skillful
> hand
> As the threads of gold and silver in the pattern He has
> planned.[2]

Asking . . . and Acting!

STEP 1: ASKING

Pruning is painful. Yet, in John 15 Jesus tells us that we will be pruned regardless of our state. If we're not growing well, we get pruned. If we're bearing fruit, we still get pruned. Knowing that the Master uses experiences that deeply cut us in the pruning process, are you willing to surrender to the Master's pruning shears so that you can bear more fruit and have more love, more joy, more peace?

STEP 2: ACTING

Take a moment right now and tell the Master that you're willing to accept pruning in your life and that you will receive His pruning for good and not for evil. Assure Him that you will continue believing He has a loving purpose for your life regardless of the severity of the pruning. Recognize that a knife in the hand of a surgeon is different from a knife in the hand of a thief. Jesus is your Great Physician.

FOR BIBLE STUDY

Genesis 3:4, 6	Matthew 11:25
Deuteronomy 29:29	Mark 4:40
2 Chronicles 7:14	Luke 16:26
Psalm 1:3	John 5:39
Proverbs 3:5	Hebrews 1:14
Isaiah 45:15	

FOURTEEN

CHARACTER BUILDING? I'LL PASS, THANKS

Trust Him . . . when doubts seem much stronger
Trust Him . . . when strength may be small
Trust Him . . . when simply to trust Him
May be the hardest thing of all.

Pain?

No, thanks. I don't want any.

Yes, I've heard it said, "No pain, no gain." And I suppose it's true. But that doesn't mean I have to like it. And I don't.

Still, I'll have to admit that there is some character building all mixed up in this suffering thing. The bottom line is that I believe God allowed just the right amount of suffering and loss in my life to accomplish His purposes in me. I assume He's not through with me yet, because what He allowed to come against me was not enough to take my life, but just enough to shake it.

If you're suffering, you may take heart from the fact that you've got plenty of company. Author Larry Burkett, who fought cancer and won, came to this conclusion:

> Although some may call it coincidence, I believe that God allowed only the amount of cancer that was necessary to perform His perfect will in my life. Apparently at that time it was not God's will for me to die from cancer. I try not to focus on why something happens; rather I focus on what God wants me to do as a result of it.[1]

Good for you, Larry! We would all do well to follow his example of looking not at the things we've lost but rather at the blessings God has given us. Larry's story made me think of a classified ad I read about. Someone was frantically looking for a lost dog, and described him like this:

LOST DOG:
BLOND GERMAN SHEPHERD,
THREE LEGS,
TAIL BROKEN,
BLIND IN ONE EYE,
LEFT EAR MISSING,
ANSWERS TO THE NAME "LUCKY."

JOSEPH: "LUCKY"?

The Old Testament character Joseph knew what it meant to suffer unjustly. The little dude hadn't done anything wrong, yet his own brothers sold him to be a slave. Talk about a bad day! There he was, minding his own business, trying to interpret the dreams God had given him, when it suddenly seems that God deserted him and allowed the worst to happen to him. Off to Egypt he went to be falsely accused of a crime and sent to prison. (And that was a prison without a workout room or a library.)

Joseph must have gone over the situation again and again in his head, especially after dark when he was tossing and turning, trying to sleep. The questions probably wouldn't go away: "What did I do wrong? Why has God forsaken me?" But somewhere in that lonely darkness, Joseph must have convinced himself that God was aware of his plight and would someday act in his behalf—and that knowledge kept him from nurturing a root of bitterness against the Lord and against his brothers.

It always astounds me when I read the Bible's account of Joseph's first reaction upon seeing his family again after over fourteen years in exile. In Genesis 45:4–5, he says: "I am your brother Joseph, the one you sold into Egypt! And now, do not be distressed and do not be angry with yourselves for selling me here, because it was to save lives that God sent me ahead of you." Even in prison, Joseph knew that God was somehow involved in his crummy circumstances.

What an amazing, forgiving spirit! He could feel that way only because he kept his eyes on God and knew that, ultimately, God was in charge of everything that happened to him and was using it to bring about good in his life. Joseph even went so far as to graciously move his father and brothers to Egypt, so they could escape the famine that had a killer-grip on Canaan and live in comfort and prosperity. He must have privately forgiven his brothers before they ever came to Egypt. Actively choosing to forgive is always part of the healing process. That enabled him to look them in the eyes and say without malice, "You meant it for evil, but God meant it for good."

Maybe you and I will never see the entire story, as Joseph did. Perhaps we'll only know our stories of struggling, without seeing the purpose or entirely understanding it all. The tragedy you're enduring right now could turn out to be just one bad chapter in the otherwise wonderful story of your life. Maybe you're just building your testimony. Please choose to believe with me, as Joseph did, that there is a bigger picture and that, as the hymn says, "we'll understand it all by and by."

So many Bible characters experienced a feeling of being abandoned by God. King David once cried, "How long, O LORD? Will you forget me forever?" (Ps. 13:1). But God has a purpose to everything He does, even when He seems to be hiding from us. As the Bible says regarding God's dealing with Hezekiah: "God left him to test him and to know everything that was in his heart" (2 Chron. 32:31). This may be the very thing God is doing with many of us today, testing us to know everything that's in our hearts.

AFFLICTIONS FOR THE APOSTLES

We've already talked about Paul's "thorn in the flesh" and how he prayed fervently to have it taken away. Paul knew what it was to have a streak of bad luck and disasters, yet he unashamedly wrote:

> I have worked much harder, been in prison more frequently, been flogged more severely, and been exposed to death again and again. Five times I received from the Jews the forty lashes minus one. Three times I was beaten with rods, once I was stoned, three times I was shipwrecked, I spent a night and a day in the open sea, I have been constantly on the move. I have been in danger from rivers, in danger from bandits, in danger from my own countrymen, in danger from Gentiles; in danger in the city, in danger in the country, in danger at sea; and in danger from false brothers. I have labored and toiled and have often gone without sleep; I have known hunger and thirst, and have often gone without food; I have been cold and naked. Besides everything else, I face daily the pressure of my concern for all the churches. Who is weak, and I do not feel weak?
>
> 2 Corinthians 11:23–29

Paul also told the Corinthians that they should "judge nothing before the appointed time" (1 Cor. 4:5). It may take some time for you to see how God will weave today's misery into a beautiful tapestry for you, but I believe He will do just that. It ain't over 'til it's over.

Yes, Paul knew all about suffering and pain. Yet he never considered turning back from following after Christ. He continued fighting the good fight up until the very day he was killed.

The other apostles also suffered tremendously for their faith. They were beaten, tortured, and eventually all of them were martyred—with the lone exception of John. They hurt, they bled, they cried out in pain. God did not put a protective fence around them, but I'm sure that today every one of those men counts his sufferings as nothing compared to the joy he knows on "the other side."

The seventh chapter of Acts records the stoning of Stephen, a man "full of the Holy Spirit." It used to be that every time I read that story I wondered why one of the apostles didn't step forward and perform a miracle to save Stephen's life. But now I can see that what actually happened was more impressive than any divine intervention. As the stones pelted his body, Stephen prayed out loud, "Lord, do not hold this sin against them" (Acts 7:59). Now that attitude was a *real* miracle.

JESUS, THE MAN OF SORROWS

Hebrews 5:8 says that our Lord learned obedience through the things He suffered. Well, if it was necessary for Christ to suffer, then how in the world can ordinary people like you and me think we shouldn't have to suffer?

I imagine that Christ's suffering began when He was still a little boy. After all, I'm sure the neighbors speculated as to who His real father was. Anyone who could add knew that Jesus was conceived before Mary and Joseph were married, and chances are the Jesus didn't look the slightest thing like his earthly stepdad. So He had to endure their stares, their ridicule, and their rude whispering.

But if He suffered as a little boy, it was mild compared to what lay ahead of Him. But whenever suffering came His way, Jesus wanted to see His Father's will done. But I can't help thinking that the Master was shaken when He received the news that his friend and cousin, John the Baptist, had been beheaded. Luke tells us that in the Garden of Gethsemane, Christ was in such emotional agony that "his sweat was like drops of blood falling to the ground" (Luke 22:44). He also told His apostles, "My soul is overwhelmed with sorrow to the point of death" (Matt. 26:38). A terrible struggle was raging inside of Him. Should He call the whole thing off? He could call on ten thousand angels to rescue Him, but He knew that He had to obey the Father's will, which was that He would have to suffer for you and me.

I benefited so much from being part of a symphony chorus that performed a great J. S. Bach oratorio, *The St. Matthew Passion*. During this time I memorized much of the Passion section from the Book of Matthew, because many of those Scriptures are contained within the oratorio's lyrics. A verse from one of those chorale numbers will always stay with me:

> When life begins to fail me,
> I fear not, having Thee.
> When pains of death assail me,
> My comfort Thou wilt be.
> When e'er from woes that grieve me,
> I seek to find relief,
> Alone Thou wilt not leave me,
> For Thou hast tasted grief.[2]

The only Son of the Living God, facing an agonizing death on the cross, was in so much agony that He prayed, "may this cup be taken from me." But it was not taken away, and our Savior suffered and died. Was His death a tragic waste? No! It was a necessary part of God's plan. Through His suffering and death, Christ became our Savior and our Helper, the One who assists us as we pass through our own pain and grief. "For since he himself has passed through the test of suffering, he is able to help those who are meeting their test now" (Heb. 2:18 NEB).

I love these words of Isaiah from Handel's *Messiah:*

> He was despised and rejected,
> a man of sorrows and acquainted with grief.
> He gave His back to the smiters,
> and His cheeks to them that plucked off the hair.
> He hid not His face from shame and spitting.

I know that I am saved because of what Christ did on the cross. But I also believe that, just as God had a plan to use His Son's sufferings for good, He also has a positive plan for us that will use our suffering—a plan that is better than anything we could devise for ourselves.

I'm certain that God's heart was breaking as He watched His Son suffer and die, especially when Jesus cried out, "My God, my God, why have You forsaken me?" But God had to provide the sacrifice of a spotless, sinless lamb for the salvation of the world. I'm sure God wanted to intervene. When Hal became ill, He had a better plan in mind than intervening. Because breast cancer was in His will for me, I have to trust that it will bring about my ultimate good. I believe all of these things were necessary for some reason, but I also believe God's heart was hurting through these difficult struggles.

RESPONDING TO SUFFERING

Admittedly, some suffering is so severe that it defies any possible explanation. It would be beyond cruel for me to

205

say that those who suffered in Nazi concentration camps were just having character built into them. Why did God allow such horror? I wouldn't presume to try to answer that question. But in Viktor Frankl's book, *Man's Search for Meaning*, he tells of watching his fellow prisoners exercise the power to decide how they would respond to their unfair circumstances. Some folks displayed inspiring dignity, courage, and inner vitality. They chose to believe in a loving God despite all of the evidence to the contrary that surrounded them.

If we allow it to, suffering can provide us with the opportunity to rethink our lives. It can cause us to check our priorities and take inventory. When Hal died, I realized that nothing would ever be "normal" again, so I had to find a "new normal." The part of me that was defined as "Hal's wife" no longer existed. I had to figure out who I was and where I was headed. I miss my mate, but through this loss I have become stronger than I was before.

You may not believe it right now, but tragedy and loss can be a positive force in your life.

I've had people say to me, "I never imagined that being fired could be the best thing that ever happened to me."

And, "Since my accident, I've found a closer walk with the Lord."

And, "When my husband left me, I never thought I could make it on my own, but now I'm discovering how strong I am, and that makes me feel good about myself."

You see: "In times of trouble, some people grow wings, others buy crutches."[3]

Are you facing a difficult situation, perhaps even a life-threatening one? Welcome. You are among a fine group who have had the opportunity to face our mortality squarely in the eye. We are better for it. There is not one survivor who doesn't admit that the diagnosis, the accident, or the struggle didn't change them. Remember, the important thing about your lot in life is whether you use it for parking or building!

MODERN-DAY WARRIORS

I know quite a few people who've grown wings. They flew through the fire of tragedy and came out the other side without so much as the smell of smoke on them.

I relived the agony of dealing with cancer as my dear friend and fellow-author Emilie Barnes battled both lymphoma and stomach cancer. She fought on when she felt like giving up and even traveled and maintained much of her national itinerary. Her courage and faith touched me deeply.

The important thing about your lot
in life is whether you use it
for parking or building!

The last time I visited her, she was in the same hospital where I had surgery and on the same floor where Hal passed away. I swallowed hard as I stepped off the elevator and realized, "I'm not going to make it through this without a little humor." I borrowed a few props from a nurse-friend and arrived in Emilie's room in a doctor's jacket, complete with a stethoscope and enema bag.

We all got a good laugh, which we needed—although Emilie's husband Bob told me later that when he saw the large syringe in my hand, he was afraid I was the proctologist's assistant coming for him!

As we visited in her room that day, we knew that God was with us. As the psalmist said, "Though I make my bed in hell, behold! Thou art there" (Ps. 139:8 KJV). How amazing! There is no place where God will not meet us.

Then there is my friend Bob, who is paralyzed and lives in an assisted-living facility. There was a time when Bob was emotionally devastated by his condition and would often ask, "Why can't I just die and go to be with Jesus?"

A tough old friend of his finally gave him the answer he needed to hear. "You know why you're still here, Bob?" he snapped. "Because you make Satan sick; isn't that great? He knows you have the capacity—from your wheelchair— to witness for Christ like nobody else can. Everyone you meet has something to learn from you. God thinks you can teach them a thing or two." Bob laughed, but that "talking-to" really helped him. Now, I believe he is accruing credits in his heavenly bank account every day.

You can't comfort without having first been uncomfortable yourself!

Paul told the church at Philippi that he wanted to "depart and be with Christ," but that "it is more necessary for you that I remain" (Phil. 1:23–24). I don't know who you are or what your condition may be. But as long as you are alive, you are capable of making a difference in this world.

Not long ago, I had an interview at a radio station in Florida. I was told ahead of time that a young girl had ditched school that day just so she could be there to meet me. The year before, at the age of eleven, she had been abducted and raped on her way to school and had become pregnant as a result of that rape. The girl had no father. Her mother was a drug addict.

With no one to guide her, she bravely contacted a local crisis pregnancy center, and there she found the compassion and care she needed. She gave birth to her baby and then gave it up for adoption. The caring folks at the crisis center keep in close touch with her, and she has become involved in a solid church, where she is growing in Christ.

She just wanted to tell me that my similar experience had given her courage. As I hugged her, I told her that she was my hero and that I believed God had a beautiful plan for her future. Her bravery and maturity amazed me.

NOT DISABLED, BUT ENABLED

One of my favorite people is Joni Eareckson Tada, who became a paraplegic as the result of a swimming accident when she was a teenager. Joni could have given in to depression and regret and spent her life in misery. Instead, she has become a well-respected artist, a best-selling author, and a witness for Christ who has touched millions of people. Joni knows what it's like to have well-meaning folks try to give her a reason for what happened to her, and she writes:

> When your heart is being wrung out like a sponge, an orderly list of "sixteen good biblical reasons as to why this is happening" can sting like salt in a wound. You don't stop the bleeding that way. A checklist may be okay when you are looking at your suffering in a rearview mirror, but when you're hurting in the present tense, "Let me explain why this is happening," isn't always livable.[4]

In an interview with *Today's Christian Woman*, Joni said, "In heaven, I look forward to folding up my wheelchair, handing it to Jesus, and saying . . . 'Thanks, I needed that!'"[5] Such a great attitude! Who says we have lost all our heroes?

GOD'S DEALERSHIP

Did God cause Joni to be involved in that terrible accident as a teenager? No! Did He cause my friend Bob to spend his life in a wheelchair? Again, no! And what about that eleven-year-old girl? Was it God's will that she should be raped? Absolutely not!

God is not the one who causes suffering. But I am afraid that in many cases it's Christians like us who allow suffering to continue. We stand idly by and watch, shaking our heads at the world's ills and waiting for the rapture. But aren't we supposed to be God's representatives?

If my Ford van breaks down, I don't try to call Henry Ford or one of his executives and complain. I take the van to a local dealership, where there are employees trained and equipped to fix the problem.

That's us. We are God's local dealership—His designated servicemen and women. When we see injustice and unfairness, we should do whatever we can to fix the situation. If a grieving widow comes to me, I'll offer her a shoulder to cry on, pass on any helpful hints I've learned, pray with her, and maybe even take her to a funny movie to lift her spirits. If a crippled man asks me to pray for his healing, I will. If healing doesn't come, then I'll do whatever else I can to help—drive him to doctors' appointments, help him get groceries, take up a collection to buy a wheelchair—*whatever* he needs that I can do.

We are God's parts and service department. Are you open for business?

There is a hymn which says that "we are His hands extended." Our hands may be imperfect and inadequate, but any hands that reach out to help in the name of Jesus can be supernaturally enabled. After all, when Jesus reaches out to us, His hands are wounded and nail-scarred from life's unfairness. But it is those marred hands that administer the healing power of God's love to the entire world!

✿ ASKING . . . AND ACTING!

STEP 1: ASKING

Can you imagine that good may come out of bad situations? Can you think of some times in your life when you thought something "bad" had happened to you, but it turned out later on to be a good thing?

STEP 2: ACTING

One of the best ways to overcome personal pain and sorrow is to reach out to others. Is there someone in your neighborhood who needs your help? An elderly widow? A stressed-out single mom? Someone who is housebound or chronically ill? Take some time to think about what you can do to ease that person's burdens. And then do it! You may find a joy that will transform your life forever!

FOR BIBLE STUDY

Genesis 45:4-5   Acts 7:59
2 Chronicles 32:31   1 Corinthians 4:5
Psalms 13:1; 139:8   2 Corinthians 11:23-29
Matthew 26:38   Philippians 1:23-24
Luke 22:44   Hebrews 2:18; 5:8

FIFTEEN

TURNING OUR WOUNDS INTO WISDOM

When God closes a door,
He opens another door . . .
But there can be a whale of a hallway in between!

Wisdom.

There is no material treasure on earth that can match the priceless value of wisdom. When the result of our wounded state is wisdom, somehow our pain becomes precious. It has not been in vain after all.

Ah . . . but it is a treacherous journey to reach wisdom's shores from the world's battlefield. Yet God's purposes are being worked out with every staggering step we take toward the door He's already opened for us. Maybe you've made it through this hallway with me. Maybe you are caught in the middle of this transition and it is dark. You are groping to find your way.

I offer my sincere apologies to you if you hoped these pages would work some kind of magic spell for you. Perhaps you hoped you'd find the reason . . . some deep, redeeming meaning in your affliction. I do not present my thoughts here as if I were the "Bible Answer Gal." I do not have all the answers. (Why, at times I barely know the questions.)

I too am a fellow struggler, and my goal is to offer you hints, clues, concepts, and principles to point you in the right direction. I intended to lure you into a deeper walk with Christ. He is the only One who can give you the satisfaction you seek.

We have arrived at the time when we must hold our heads high and choose, in spite of our unanswered queries, to stop our incessant questioning. Let us determine to pick up our cross and follow Him—not with a "poor me, I'm a victim" attitude but rather as a devoted soldier who trusts the integrity of the Leader he fights with.

Yes, it is time to move on. To make progress at last. So much of our desperate questioning remains a mystery, and as Paul says, we must be faithful stewards of the "secret things" entrusted to us by God (see 1 Cor. 4:1). Suffering is one of those hidden mysteries. When you are caught in it, I encourage you to make choices that lead to growth and life. Take heart, for as Peter reminds us:

> The suffering won't last forever. It won't be long before this generous God who has great plans for us in Christ—eternal and glorious plans they are!—will have you put together and on your feet for good.
>
> 1 Peter 5:10 Message

The Bridge over Troubled Waters

As we go through life, we will weather many storms. Sometimes it will be a physical storm, governed by natural phenomena. Other times, Satan will hurl one at us when he catches us off guard. (Honestly, though, we often stir up our own storms!)

It's good to keep in mind that it was during times of trouble that Jesus would show up. When there was a need and a willing heart, He was there. Remember?

- When a cripple asked for help.
- When a widow's only son died.
- When the disciples couldn't catch one single fish.
- When a crowd was hungry.
- When gales of wind and torrents of rain tossed His terrified disciples around on a stormy sea.
- When His friend Lazarus died, and Jesus showed His power in a miraculous way.

When stormy troubles overtake us, we will weather them well if we remember He is with us. And ultimately the storm will show us:

- The level of our maturity.
- Our understanding of God's character.
- The strength and depth of our commitment.
- How hair-trigger our anger is.
- How teachable we are.
- Whether our attitude is to surrender or to fight.

When the storm subsides, we must mop up! We can then see what kind of foundation our faith is built upon. Is it unstable and sandy . . . or solidly built on the Rock? We can reinforce shutters that blew loose. Things that were tossed about can be repaired. Our house of faith can be stronger than ever before.

As we discussed in chapter 12, this process of struggle can be likened also to the pruning process. Pruning, you say? That means cutting away, doesn't it? Ouch! No thanks. I wish there were some less invasive way to bear more fruit, but there isn't.

Have you been resisting God's pruning process? Stop right now and tell Him you accept the pruning in your life. Thank Him for using it for good and not for evil and assure Him you still believe in His loving purpose for you . . . in spite of everything.

WOUNDED HEALERS

Ever notice how God delights to use folks who are scarred . . . people with a limp? His most useful workers are those who have been through it all and made it to the other side. These are the ones His light shines brightly through— like a blazing fire. Author Patsy Clairmont knew what she was talking about when she titled her delightful book *God Uses Cracked Pots*. It's not the perfect ones who have lived a charmed life who can reflect the glory of God. It's the ones who have taken a few hard hits and have had their own imperfect exterior "cracked open" so that He can use them as vessels for Christ's light to shine through.

Choose, by faith, to create a new life within this unexpected framework!

Wounded healer, hang on to your belief that God is good. He still loves you, as He loved Jesus when Jesus agonized through His human sufferings.

Your mourning, questioning experience does not innately have the power to separate you from God. It is your choice, and if you choose to isolate yourself from God, you will miss the one true source of consolation and healing. Hear these encouraging words from the apostle Paul, recorded in Romans 8:38–39:

> For I am convinced that neither death nor life, neither angels nor demons, neither the present nor the future, nor any powers, neither height nor depth, nor anything else in all creation, will be able to separate us from the love of God that is in Christ Jesus our Lord.

No Answer Yet?

When you cry out to God and there is no immediate answer, does it mean He is not listening? Does it mean He does not care? No, let us use those times to grow in godly character. God's answer could be "on hold" for reasons He is not obliged to explain to us. Don't assume He is saying "no" when He may be saying "wait and see." We're safe when we submit ourselves to God's timing. Let's factor in that this may be a test . . . no, an *opportunity* to experience God's peace. In spite of crummy circumstances! After all, God hasn't taught us to swim just to let us drown. The following words from Isaiah 43:1–2 can encourage us greatly if we remember to claim them in a trial. If you find inspirational music to be a soothing comfort, the sentiments in these verses are beautifully sung by recording artist Pam Rozell.

> Fear not, for I have redeemed you;
>   I have called you by name; you are mine.
> When you pass through the waters,
>   I will be with you;
> and when you pass through the rivers,
>   they will not sweep over you.
> When you walk through the fire,
>   you will not be burned;
>   and the flames will not set you ablaze.[1]

217

BEFORE PASSING JUDGMENT . . . GIVE IT TIME

Perhaps at this very minute you are reading this book and feeling that the cross you bear today is the most devastating experience of your life. Remember, it's not over yet!

A dear Christian man in Canada told me a strange tale about his family that may help put things in perspective for you. This gentleman was a farmer who had lost his only horse. Everyone said, "How sad, you lost your only horse."

He replied, "But how do you know this is a bad thing?"

The very next day his horse returned, with six wild horses in tow! The farmer ran to open his corral to secure his now bursting stable of seven healthy horses.

"That's great!" exclaimed the neighbors.

"But how do you know this is a good thing?" asked the farmer.

The very next day the farmer's only son was trying to tame one of the wild horses and was thrown off. His leg was broken in three places, which caused the watchful friends to remark, "How sad! Your son will be unable to work and have to wear a cast for weeks."

The farmer thought about it a moment and replied, "But how do you know this is a bad thing?"

Ironically enough, the son was scheduled to report for an Army recruiting physical that week. Guess what? His broken leg disqualified him from eligibility to enlist.

Again the neighbors rejoiced. "Great!" they exclaimed. "Now your son will never go to war."

"But how can you be sure this is a great blessing?" asked the father. His question was almost prophetic, since the son sadly became a prodigal. Yet, when he was converted later in life, he had a marvelous testimony of God's always watching over him.

The point of this story, my suffering friend, is to make you aware that it may be way too early to judge whether or not this catastrophe in your life will ultimately be devastating.

Perhaps you will soon see how God is working it into His plan for you! Both the good and bad may be woven together into the beautiful tapestry of your life. As the old hymn puts it:

> He whose heart is kind beyond all measure
> Gives unto each day what He deems best.
> Lovingly, it's part of pain or pleasure,
> Mingling toil with peace and rest.

STRENGTH FOR TODAY, BRIGHT HOPE FOR TOMORROW

Another parable tells of a farmer whose mule fell into the well. Calculating the impossibility of this situation, the farmer decided it would be an act of compassion to bury the mule. His farmhands began shoveling dirt in the well to put the frantic mule out of his misery.

As the dirt began to fall on the animal, his instincts told him to "Shake it off and step up on it." Shake and step . . . shake and step . . . every time a load would fall on the mule's back, he would respond this way. It was not long before the mule's head could be seen sticking out of the well, much to the amazement of the workers shoveling dirt.

Life can be approached with the same tenacity of that old mule. Adversities come dumping down on us, seeming to bury us alive. They could too if we let them. But we have a choice. We can use them for our benefit by shaking them off and using them as stepping-stones. Step right up!

Since my bout with cancer, folks are always asking me how I'm doing these days. Am I over it all? I doubt it. I have only the strength I need for today. My struggling as a widow continues, and with my family history of cancer, I live daily with the threat of recurrence. Yet, though I feel broken, I also feel strangely whole. In my weakest and most vulnerable moments, God's Spirit convinces me that my strength, stability, and soundness of mind is all tied up in Christ.

It may sound strange now that you've heard my story, but I still believe God can use me to pray effectively for someone who is sick. If I am clean before God and I'm simply at the right place in His right time, I trust He could use me to minister healing to someone else. How I'd love to return to the pediatric oncology ward where I entertained kids. What a joy it would be to feel the moving of God's Spirit inside me and say to a child there, "Silver and gold have I none, but such as I have I give to you. Turn around, take up your bed, and walk out of here well and whole!"

Still, I wouldn't dare to do this without the inner assurance that God's anointing for healing rested upon me. But the point I am making is that our own endurance of pain and sickness does not disqualify us as vessels of His healing to others. Actually, your struggles may be the very thing that qualifies you to help others. I must keep moving on with God, trying to interpret and perceive the new things He has in store. I love these words from Isaiah 43:18–19:

> Forget the former things;
> do not dwell on the past.
> See, I am doing a new thing!
> Now it springs up; do you not perceive it?

You may know the story of how Elisabeth Elliot's husband was martyred serving God as a missionary. If anyone ever had a case against God, it's her. Yet she writes that "only in acceptance lies peace, not in resignation."[2] Like Elisabeth Elliot, I had somehow arrived at a place of acceptance. My questions are not all answered. My scars remain. My wounds can still be opened by a nostalgic memory. But I have accepted what has happened to me as part of God's

plan for my life. I do not understand why, but I trust Him
. . . because He is trustworthy.

Maybe Our Prayers Have Been Answered?

Let's be Pain Pals! What have we learned from our questionings? I hope you feel content, as I now do, to leave the hidden things of God—His mysteries—in His hands. If you have cried out to Him, believe He has answered—even if your experiences seem to contradict that.

Never forget: God loves you more than anyone else could ever possibly love you.

And He is in control.

We can rest now.

🌿 ASKING . . . AND ACTING!

STEP 1: ASKING

In all of your questioning, have you neglected to ask the one most important question of all? Have you asked Jesus Christ to be Savior and Lord of your life?

STEP 2: ACTING

If you have never received Christ into your heart, you will never sit with God in His throne room and hear His answers to your questions. If you have not done so, drop to your knees right now and sincerely pray the following prayer:

Lord God Almighty,
I confess that I am a sinner.
I do not deserve Your mercy,
But I believe You give it freely.
To receive it, I know I must acknowledge that Jesus died
    in my place.
My sins were laid upon Him as He died on the cross.
Thank You, Jesus.
I receive Your gift of salvation today.
Come into my heart now
And be my Savior and Lord forever.
Amen!

FOR BIBLE STUDY

Isaiah 43:1–2; 18–19
Romans 8:38–39
1 Corinthians 4:1
1 Peter 5:10

CANCER APPENDIX

CANCER INSIGHTS FROM THE AUTHOR

Although I am not a physician, I'd like to pass on a few things I've learned to help cancer patients and caregivers.

What causes cancer? Volumes have been written about this, but the list of contributing factors may include:

genetics/heredity
exposure to radiation
drugs
chemicals in water
excessive alcohol
chronic stress
a diet high in fat and protein

toxic chemicals
pesticides
excessive caffeine
tobacco products
estrogen
unresolved conflict

One good thing about the "health nuts" (as I used to call them) is that they are consistent; they readily agree on the basics of what it takes to be healthy.

Diet and exercise. Many sources warn that one-third of the fight against returning cancer involves exercise! Before my bout with cancer I never exercised. (The only exercise I got was stretching the truth, pushing my luck, and carrying a grudge!) But my research has convinced me that proper physical exercise, along with good food intake (boosted with supplements—vitamins, minerals, etc.) is essential to help the immune system fight off a recurrence of cancer.

Americans (especially) have been deceived about food. We live out Proverbs 23:1–3:

> When you sit down to dine with a ruler,
>   note well what is before you,
> and put a knife to your throat
>   if you are given to gluttony.
> Do not crave his delicacies,
>   for that food is deceptive.

The catch is (sorry about this) that the foods that look so tantalizing and tempting are usually the ones most lacking in good nutrition. I think God had a more simple plan for our health from the start. (After all, Adam and Eve didn't shoot turkeys and cows for food, and I'm sure Jesus never ate chicken McNuggets.) The wrong foods can seriously damage your immune system, which is your only line of defense against disease.

Most of us have neglected and abused our bodies, and that's not right. As the Bible says, our bodies are the temple of God. It's time to repent, and I'll do it with you. Ease into good nutrition. At least get started in that right direction. If we shoot for the moon . . . we may hit the trees anyhow!

WHAT ABOUT CHEMOTHERAPY?

By my count there are at least 110 chemotherapy drugs currently available. Although many of these chemicals are still being tested by the FDA, they are being widely used. The FDA's reluctance to approve the drugs is due to the high degree of toxicity (poison) necessary to kill off cancer cells. This potency became evident to me when one nurse could not get the needle properly inserted into Hal's arm. When the chemotherapy drug spilled out onto his skin, there was a near-panic in the room as nurses scurried to stop the problem. The toxic burn the spill left on Hal's skin never did heal.

Different cancers respond to various combinations of these drugs. And the side effects vary just as widely between patients. When you mingle all these variables, you can imagine how difficult it is for a physician to get the right protocol for a specific patient. I feel that anyone facing traditional cancer treatments should maintain a positive attitude toward their effectiveness. Many former cancer patients will tell you that chemotherapy saved their lives. So I wouldn't advise anyone to throw out traditional medical techniques, nor alternative or complementary ones. If you can integrate both into a cancer wellness program, you are in the right groove.

Author Greg Anderson understands this well. Now leading the Cancer Conquerors organization, he was once told by doctors that his cancer had progressed so far that he had only about thirty days to live. Today, years later, he is alive and well, and writes in his book *The Cancer Conqueror:*

> Personal responsibility for health means refusing to be a victim. It means participation in recovery by recognizing and changing self-destructive beliefs and behavior. This means believing I am in charge of my cancer; my cancer is not in charge of me.[1]

I would advise any cancer patient to decide to take charge of their own wellness. Ask for copies of all bloodwork and tests. This is bothersome to the doctor's staff, so you must be patient and assertive to get these. Ask questions, take notes, and listen to the nurses! They'll give you the skinny when the doctors are too preoccupied. (One kind nurse advised me, "Always be sure the same lab does your bloodwork; otherwise you can never be sure the results are accurate." That proved to be an invaluable piece of information.) The staff was not always happy to see this "humor therapist" come through their doors, because they knew I'd be loaded with questions and requests. But I was not in a popularity contest!

The following cancer testimonies are from the book *Silver Linings*, published by Oncology Nursing Press, Pittsburgh, 1997:

Soon after my breast cancer surgery, when I awoke on Christmas morning, I couldn't find my prosthesis. Searching for it had become a family joke. I gave a yell, "Has anybody seen my breast?" Then my nine-year-old daughter came in, explaining she knew how much I hated the cold prosthesis, so she had put it underneath the covers in her waterbed so it would be warm for me this Christmas morning. As I hugged her, I realized cancer can teach a family how to react to the valleys in life.

—Kathleen

Cancer separates us from other people. We hear our meters ticking. Joining this involuntary sisterhood of breast cancer survivors brought me to support group meetings. Sharing thoughts and emotions sheds clarity on individual situations and options. We gain strength by processing our terror, fear, ignorance and knowledge. We laugh and cry to heal ourselves.

—Karen

I saw the screen flash "search topic" and typed in "breast cancer." Much to my surprise a long list of women popped up. I could pull up profiles on women, and I found two who were willing to e-mail me, and we began a cyber friendship that lasts to this day.

—Wanda

Know someone fighting cancer? Keep in touch! When you withdraw, it sends a message to the cancer warrior that you've given up on them. Cancer victims need a steady diet of hope!

But what do you say? Be as positive as possible. It's okay to ask how they are doing. Let them know you are praying for them. Tell them you want to help in specific ways. Can you drive them to or from treatment? Do they need washing done? Would a trip to the market help? This practical help—and you just being yourself—may be your greatest gift to the cancer struggler.

CANCER RESOURCES

This list is being provided for readers dealing with cancer or cancer patients. The author does not necessarily endorse any advice or counsel given by the following resources, but provides it for your own research and information.

Information by Phone/Internet:

American Cancer Society	800-ACS-2345 www.cancer.org
Cancer Information Service	800-4-CANCER www.cancernet.nci
Reach to Recovery	212-237-2849
American Institute for Cancer Research	800-843-8114 www.aicr.org
National Alliance of Breast Cancer Organizations	212-889-0606 www.nabco.org
Compassionate Friends	708-990-0010

Recommended Reading on Cancer

I'm Alive and the Doctor's Dead, by Sue Buchanan, Zondervan

Damaged But Not Broken, by Larry Burkett, Moody Press

Conquering Cancer, by Dr. Paul Johnson, Zondervan

The Cancer Conqueror, by Greg Anderson, Universal Press Syndicate

Encourage Me: Caring Words for Heavy Hearts, by Charles Swindoll, Walker and Company

Love, Medicine and Miracles, by Dr. Bernie Siegel, Harper & Row

Anatomy of an Illness, by Norman Cousins, W. W. Norton & Company

The Cancer Answer, by Maureen Salaman, Statford Publishers

Food: Your Miracle Medicine, by Jean Carver, Harper Collins

An Alternative Medicine Definitive Guide to Cancer, by W. John Diamond, Nathaniel Mead, and Burton Goldberg, Future Medicine Publishers

The Cancer Industry, by Ralph Moss, Paragon Publishers

Encyclopedia of Natural Medicine, by Michael Murray and J. Pizzorno, Prima Publishers

Third Opinion, by John M. Fink, Avery Publishers

WIDOW'S APPENDIX

Eighty percent of wives will become widows.

AUTHOR'S INSIGHTS

If you are grieving over the loss of your spouse, it is normal to feel that your life is out of control. You will battle depression and anger. Making decisions will be strenuous. You'll find your energy level is low. All this is natural—and it is temporary. You will regain control of your life.

In processing my own grief and mourning, I found Scripture to be such an encouragement! If you have lost a spouse, take heart from God's promises to you:

"Remember no more the reproach of your widowhood. For your Maker is your husband—the LORD Almighty is his name" (Isa. 54:4–5).

"Do not take advantage of a widow" (Exod. 22:22).

"He defends the cause of the . . . widow" (Deut. 10:18).

"Do not . . . take the cloak of the widow as a pledge" (Deut. 24:17).

"Cursed is the man who withholds justice from the . . . widow" (Deut. 27:19).

"The LORD . . . sustains the fatherless and the widow" (Ps. 146:9).

"The widow who is really in need and left all alone puts her hope in God and continues night and day to pray and to ask God for help" (1 Tim. 5:5–6).

Also, see 1 Kings 17:7–24 for an encouraging story of an encounter between a poor widow and the prophet Elijah. See Mark 12:42–44 for Jesus' thoughts on a widow's small gift to the temple, and Luke 18:1–8 for His parable of the persistent widow.

MAKING PLANS

I would highly recommend to every wife that she be quietly and wisely prepared for the passing of her husband. I regret that I was totally unprepared for this tragic inevitability. If your husband is currently healthy, this is the easiest time for you to find answers to the following questions. In any case, the time to gather the information you need is now.

Do you know if your husband prefers burial or cremation?
Do you know his desires for a memorial service? His preference for music, remarks?
Where would he like to be buried?
Have you made plot arrangements?
Do you know the wording he wants on his headstone?
Which funeral home will you use?
Does he want his casket open or closed during his funeral?
Did you know you can prepay all funeral expenses? (What a blessing this would be for your family!)
Does your husband have a will? A living will?
Where is it located? What attorney will handle this will? Do you have the attorney's name, address, and phone number?
Are you your husband's sole beneficiary?

Can you locate your health insurance policy? Does it include death benefits?

Can you locate your life insurance papers? How many different policies do you have?

Is the beneficiary listed the same as on his will?

Make a list of the policies and contacts.

What is the total amount of these policies?

Is this money taxable?

What loans remain to be paid?

Is there death insurance on any of these?

Do you know how much your social security benefits will be?

In the case of a second marriage, do you have a pre-nuptial agreement?

Do you know if your husband's will will have to go through probate?

Would you need employment if your husband were no longer here?

How much income will you need per month to meet your current obligations?

If you own your own home, do you have a mortgage?

Is there death insurance on this mortgage?

Where do you do your banking?

Make a list of all your accounts.

Are all accounts in both names?

Do you have a safe-deposit box? If so, is it in both your names? Do you know where the key is?

Is there one particular person you could rely on for financial advice?

If you have dependents, do you have money set aside for their education?

Does your spouse have any feelings about your remarrying?

Are you assured you will see your husband again in heaven? (If not, there's no time like the present to talk to him about the importance of faith in Christ.)

One thing I urge you to do above all others: Begin to treat your husband in such a way that you would be perfectly at peace if he met God before you saw him again!

RECOMMENDED READING

A *Grace Disguised*, by Gerald Sittser, Zondervan

Grief Is a Family Affair, by Marilyn Heavilin, Here's Life Publishers

Where Is God When It Hurts? by Philip Yancey, Zondervan

When God Weeps, by Joni Eareckson Tada, Zondervan

When God Doesn't Make Sense, by Dr. James Dobson, Tyndale House

Sandy: A Heart for God, by Leighton Ford, InterVarsity Press

Getting to the Other Side of Grief, by Susan Zonnebelt-Smeenge and Robert C. DeVries, Baker Book House

Also, check out this web site: GriefResource.com

NOTES

CHAPTER 2: DEALING WITH THE "BIG C"

1. Larry Burkett, *Damaged But Not Broken* (Chicago: Moody Press, 1996), 81.

2. Sidney J. Winawer, *Healing Lessons* (New York: Little, Brown and Company, 1998), 3.

CHAPTER 5: FAITH . . . OR PRESUMPTION?

1. Quoted in *Christianity Today*, April 27, 1998, 93.

2. James Van Tholen, "Surprised by Death," *Christianity Today*, May 21, 1999, 57.

CHAPTER 6: GRACE AT DEATH'S DOOR

1. Donald S. McCrossan, "On the Jericho Road," Hill & Range Songs, Inc.

2. William Shakespeare, "The Presence of the Absence."

CHAPTER 7: SEEK AND YE SHALL FIND

1. Erwin W. Lutzer, *One Minute After You Die* (Chicago: Moody Press, 1997), 63, 65.

2. Randy Alcorn, *Dominion* (Sisters, Oreg.: Multnomah Press, 1996), 226.

CHAPTER 8: GRACE COMES IN THE MOURNING

1. Gerald Sittser, *A Grace Disguised* (Grand Rapids: Zondervan, 1995), 19.

CHAPTER 9: AFTERSHOCK

1. The Martins, "There's Not a Crown without a Cross" (Geron Davis/ Bob Farrell/ Birdwing Music/BMG Songs, Inc.). Used by permission.

2. Sue Buchanan, *I'm Alive and the Doctor's Dead* (Grand Rapids: Zondervan, 1994), 2.

3. Peggy McCarthy and Jo An Loren, *Breast Cancer?* (Grand Rapids: Zondervan, 1994), 192.

4. Ibid., xi.

CHAPTER 10: THE ROLLER COASTER OF LIFE

1. *The Encourager Newsletter*, Vol. 5, No. 3, Summer 1999, 2, published by Dave Dravecky's Outreach of Hope.

CHAPTER 11: FAITH TAKES TIME

1. Philip Yancey, *Disappointment with God* (Grand Rapids: Zondervan, 1988), 143.

2. Paul Brand and Philip Yancey, *The Gift of Pain* (Grand Rapids: Zondervan, 1993), 272.

3. Don Stephens, *Mandate for Mercy* (Lindale, Tex.: YWAM Publishers, 1995), 23.

4. Laura Schlesinger, *Dr. Laura Schlesinger's Day Calendar* (New York: Harper Collins, 1999), June 20.

Chapter 12: When It Rains It Pours

1. C. S. Lewis, quoted by Ronald Knox in "Let Dons Delight," *Christianity Today*, April 28, 1998, 93.

2. From the song "Seasons of the Soul" by Jamie Owens Collins, © 1996 Fairhill Music. Used by permission.

3. John Sanders, *The God Who Risks* (Downers Grove, Ill.: InterVarsity Press, 1998), 263.

4. C. S. Lewis, *The Problem of Pain* (New York: MacMillan Publishing Company, 1962), 79.

5. *The Encourager Newsletter*, Vol. 5, No. 3, Summer 1999, 2, published by Dave Dravecky's Outreach of Hope.

6. Max Lucado, *In the Eye of the Storm* (Waco, Tex.: Word Publishers, 1991), 161–62.

Chapter 13: Fruit from the Tree of Life

1. Elisabeth Elliot in *Keep a Quiet Heart*, quoted in *Christianity Today*, June 14, 1999, 84.

2. *Running on Empty* by Annie Chapman, p. 45.

Chapter 14: Character Building? I'll Pass, Thanks

1. Larry Burkett, *Damaged But Not Broken* (Chicago: Moody Press, 1996), 8.

2. *The Passion According to St. Matthew*, J. S. Bach Vocal Score (New York: G. Schirmer, Inc., 1905), 19.

3. Verdell Davis, *Let Me Grieve, But Not Forever* (Waco, Tex.: Word Books, 1944), 129.

4. Joni Eareckson Tada, *When God Weeps* (Grand Rapids: Zondervan, 1997), 124.

5. Joni Eareckson Tada, *Today's Christian Woman* interview, September 1997, 118.

Chapter 15: Turning Our Wounds into Wisdom

1. "I Am The Lord Your God," taken from Isaiah 43:1–4, written by Walt Harrah, sung by Pam Rozell on her album *For Such a Time as This*.

2. Quoted by Catherine Marshall in *Beyond Ourselves* (New York: McGraw-Hill, 1961), 103.

Cancer Appendix

1. Greg Anderson, *The Cancer Conqueror* (Kansas City: Andrews & McMeel, 1990), 88.

Other books by Lee Ezell
   The Cinderella Syndrome
   The Missing Piece
   Pills for Parents in Pain
   Iron Jane
   Will the Real Me Please Stand Up
   Porcupine People

To get in touch with the author and/or for information on scheduling Lee to speak for an event, contact:

Lee Ezell
Box 7475
Newport Beach, CA 92658
Phone: 949-720-1919
Fax: 949-640-1811
Email: leeezell@aol.com
Web site: www.leeezell.com

Lee Ezell has come a long way since her beginnings as a child of alcoholic parents, raised in Philadelphia's inner city.

Living in Southern California now, Lee is an internationally sought-after Christian speaker, appearing at schools, special events, and churches of all denominations. She has authored eight books, which have been translated into fourteen languages.

Using her background in musical comedy to open doors for the gospel, Lee blends humor with biblical truth as she offers practical solutions to problems and shares God's message of hope. Her entertaining speaking style endears her to audiences, as she imaginatively shares on topics geared to help improve our personal relationships. Often referred to as a "humor therapist," Lee also speaks with a wealth of empathy and spiritual sensitivity. Lee loves God and loves people—and it shows. She truly is "a speaker with spark . . . who'll light a fire in your heart."